Simplicity's

QUICK & EASY SEWING FOR THE HOME

BED & BATH

Simplicity's

QUICK & EASY SEWING FOR THE HOME

BED & BATH

EDITED BY ANNE MARIE SOTO

AND THE

STAFF OF THE SIMPLICITY PATTERN COMPANY

Rodale Press, Inc.
Emmaus, Pennsylvania

© 1997 by Simplicity Pattern Company, Inc.

Published by Rodale Press, Inc.

Originally published as a hardcover edition in 1995.

SIMPLICITY

Editor: Anne Marie Soto
Contributing Editors: Peggy Bendel and Janis Bullis
Cover and Interior Designer: Christine Swirnoff
Art Direction and Production: Ripinsky & Company
Administrative Manager: Cheryl Dick
Senior Illustrator: Phoebe Gaughan
Illustrator: Deborah Sottile
Copy Editor: Didi Charney
Senior Vice President, Product, Simplicity Patterns: Judy Raymond

RODALE HOME AND GARDEN BOOKS

Editor: Susan Weaver
Designer: Patricia Field
Copy Editor: Carolyn Mandarano
Manufacturing Coordinator: Jodi Schaffer
Managing Editor, Sewing Books: Cheryl Winters-Tetreau
Editorial Director: Margaret J. Lydic
Editor-in-Chief: William Gottlieb

On the cover: Sweet Dreams, page 10

We're happy to hear from you.
For questions or comments concerning the editorial content of this book, please write to:
Rodale Press, Inc.
Book Readers' Service
33 East Minor Street
Emmaus, PA 18098

For more information about Rodale Press and the books and magazines we publish, visit our World Wide Web site at:
http://www.rodalepress.com

ISBN 0–87596–965–8   paperback

The Library of Congress has cataloged the hardcover edition as follows:

Simplicity's quick & easy sewing for the home. Bed & bath / edited by Anne Marie Soto
and the staff of the Simplicity Pattern Company.
p. cm.
ISBN 0–87596–660–8 hardcover
1. Household linens. 2. Machine sewing. 3. Bedrooms.
4. Bathrooms. I. Soto, Anne Marie. II. Simplicity Pattern Co.
III. Title: Simplicity's quick & easy sewing for the home.
TT387.S548 1995
646.2'1—dc20   95–5260

Distributed in the book trade by St. Martin's Press

2 4 6 8 10 9 7 5 3 1 paperback

CONTENTS

INTRODUCTION

Do you know that the average person spends more than four months a year in his or her bedroom? With the proliferation of televisions, telephones, exercise equipment, and the like, the modern bedroom has evolved into an all-purpose retreat—a place where one can escape, without ever having to leave home. As a result, the bedroom is no longer the last place to benefit from one's decorating skills. In fact, today's bedrooms and baths are often decorated first—before other, more public, spaces—in the house.

On the pages that follow, we've gathered together some of our favorite decorating ideas for bed and bath—in all, 34 projects. Some are photographed individually; others are grouped together to illustrate how, working one project at a time, you can ultimately transform an entire room. Some are totally at-the-sewing-machine projects, while others take advantage of easy, fabric-based craft techniques. A stenciled floral design magically changes standard sheets and pillowcases into designer-quality bed linens. A child-friendly teddy bear appliqué turns a ho-hum shower curtain and purchased towels into delightful bathroom accessories. Minimal sewing converts purchased sheets into ultra-easy pillows, duvet cover, and draped canopy.

As we developed this book, our goal was to provide the easiest and best possible instructions for these beautiful projects. That's why each full-page, four-color photograph is followed by complete, self-contained instructions, including a supply list with fabric suggestions and yardage requirements, cutting directions, and sewing and/or crafting directions. All dust ruffles and bedcoverings include instructions for customizing them to twin-size, double, queen-size, or king-size beds.

For easy reference, the book is divided into three parts. "Bedtime Stories" contains pillows, shams, comforters, duvets, and dust ruffles for everyone in the family, from baby on up. "Bath Time" is devoted exclusively to projects for the bathroom: three different shower curtains, plus embellished towels and bath mats. "Hold It!" is a collection of fabric-based accessories for bed or bath—perfect for your own home or as housewarming gifts for special friends.

"Sew Simple" tips, scattered throughout the book, contain information on tools and techniques for achieving professional results with minimal effort. Some of these tips focus on a specific project; others will help you sew faster and easier, regardless of the project.

"Design Plus" tips focus on ways to maximize the design potential of a specific project by simply changing the fabric, the color, or the trim. In this series, we also share some general tips from professional interior designers for planning the best possible decor.

"Terms & Techniques" at the back of this book contains additional helpful information. Included in this section are stitching terms, general stenciling directions, machine appliqué techniques, instructions on how to apply piping, directions on how to gather and attach a ruffle, and tips on how to achieve perfectly matched seams on fabrics that have a repeating motif. When your selected project utilizes any of these techniques, the instructions will refer you directly to the appropriate "Terms & Techniques" page.

Here's to the most beautiful bedrooms and baths around!

Simplicity Pattern Company

BEDTIME STORIES

Feminine touches abound in this beautiful bedroom ensemble—complete with gathered bed skirt, comforter, and three pillow styles.

SWEET DREAMS

RUFFLED PILLOW SHAM

Size:

20″ × 26″ (51cm × 66cm) (excluding the double ruffle)

SUPPLIES

- 2¼ yards (2.1m) of 45″ to 54″ (115cm to 138cm) wide decorator fabric, such as chintz, sateen, or polished cotton
- 6⅞ yards (6.3m) of 3½″ (9cm) wide flat eyelet trim
- 2⅝ yards (2.5m) of contrasting covered piping
- ⅝ yard (0.6m) of polyester batting
- One 20″ × 26″ (51cm × 66cm) standard-size bed pillow

CUTTING DIRECTIONS

All measurements include ½″ (1.3cm) seam allowances.

From the decorator fabric, cut:

- One 21″ × 27″ (53.5cm × 68.5cm) sham front
- Two 19″ × 21″ (48.5cm × 53.5cm) sham backs
- Six 5½″ × 42″ (14cm × 107cm) ruffle sections

From the batting, cut one 21″ × 27″ (53.5cm × 68.5cm) rectangle.

❖ DESIGN PLUS

For printed fabrics with a large design motif, cut the sham front or pillow cover front so that the motif is centered. For added dimension, outline the motif with machine stitching after the batting is basted in place.

SEWING DIRECTIONS

1 Preparing the front

Pin the batting rectangle to the wrong side of the sham front. Machine baste the layers together ⅜″ (1cm) from the raw edges, as shown in **Diagram 1**.

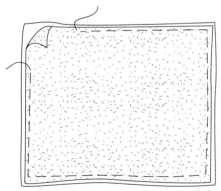

Diagram 1

On the right side of the sham front, machine baste the piping in place around the edges, following the directions on page 126 for applying piping.

2 Assembling the double ruffle

With right sides together, stitch the six ruffle sections together at the ends to form one continuous ruffle, as shown in **Diagram 2**. Press the seams open. Press under ½″ (1.3cm) on one long edge. Tuck the raw edge in to meet the crease. Press again. Stitch close to the second fold.

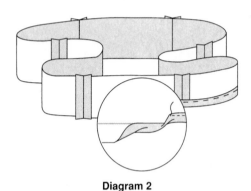

Diagram 2

With right sides together, stitch the ends of the eyelet together, as shown in **Diagram 3**. Press the seam open.

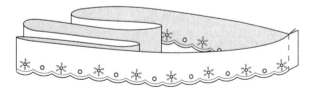

Diagram 3

🧵 SEW SIMPLE

When stitching a piped seam, stitch with the piped section on top so you can make sure the basting stitches remain inside the seam allowance.

Pin the eyelet to the ruffle, with the wrong side of the eyelet to the right side of the ruffle and raw edges even. Machine baste the layers together, as shown in **Diagram 4**, following the directions on page 125 for preparing a ruffle.

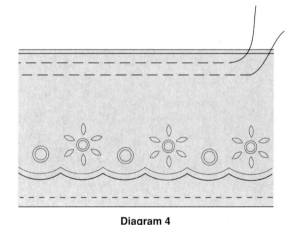

Diagram 4

3 Attaching the double ruffle

Divide and mark the double ruffle into eight equal parts.

Divide and mark the edges of the sham front into eight equal parts.

Referring to **Diagram 5,** with right sides together, baste the double ruffle to the sham front, following the directions on page 125 for gathering and attaching a ruffle. Using the sewing machine zipper foot attachment, baste through all the layers, crowding the stitches close to the piping cord.

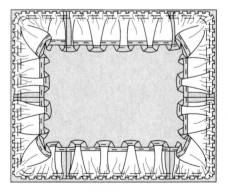

Diagram 5

4 Finishing the sham

Referring to **Diagram 6,** press under ¼" (6mm) on one short end of one sham back. Press under again 1½" (3.8cm). Stitch close to the first fold. Repeat for the other sham back.

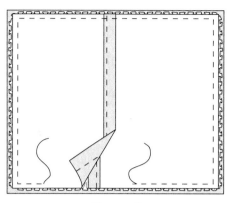

Diagram 7

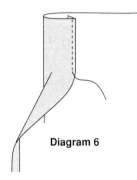

Diagram 6

Referring to **Diagram 7,** with right sides together, pin the sham backs to the sham front so that the

back finished edges overlap. Using the sewing machine zipper foot attachment, stitch around the entire outer edge of the sham, crowding the stitches as close as possible to the piping cord. Trim the corners on the diagonal and trim the seam allowances.

Turn the sham right side out. Remove the basting stitches from the ruffle. Insert the pillow.

RUFFLED PILLOW COVER

Size:

12" (30.5cm) square (excluding the ruffle)

SUPPLIES

- *1 yard (1m) of 45" to 54" (115cm to 138cm) wide decorator fabric, such as chintz, sateen, or polished cotton*
- *⅜ yard (0.4m) of polyester batting*
- *One 12" (30.5cm) square pillow form*

CUTTING DIRECTIONS

All measurements include ½" (1.3cm) seam allowances.

From the decorator fabric, cut:

- *One 13" (33cm) square cover front*
- *Two 11¼" × 13" (28.5cm × 33cm) cover backs*
- *Three 5½" × 42"(14cm × 107cm) ruffle sections*

From the batting, cut one 13" (33cm) square.

SEWING DIRECTIONS

1 Preparing the front

Pin the batting square to the wrong side of the cover front. Machine baste the layers together

⅜″ (1cm) from the raw edges, as shown in **Diagram 1.**

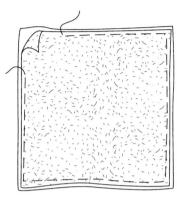

Diagram 1

2 Assembling the ruffle

With right sides together, stitch the three ruffle sections together at the ends to form one continuous ruffle, as shown in **Diagram 2.** Press the seams open. Press under ½″ (1.3cm) on one long edge. Tuck the raw edge in to meet the crease. Press again. Stitch close to the second fold.

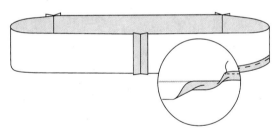

Diagram 2

Machine baste along the raw edge, following the directions on page 125 for preparing a ruffle.

3 Attaching the ruffle

Divide and mark the ruffle into eight equal parts.

Divide and mark the edges of the cover front into eight equal parts.

Referring to **Diagram 3,** with right sides together, baste the ruffle to the cover front, following the directions on page 125 for gathering and attaching a ruffle.

Diagram 3

4 Finishing the cover

Referring to **Diagram 4,** press under ¼″ (6mm) on one short end of one cover back. Press under again 1½″ (3.8cm). Stitch close to the first fold. Repeat for the other cover back.

Referring to **Diagram 5,** with right sides together, pin the backs to the front so that the finished edges of the backs overlap. Stitch ½″ (1.3cm) from the cut edge all around the cover. Trim the corners on the diagonal and trim the seam allowances.

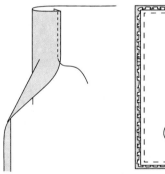
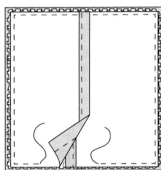

Diagram 4　　　　　　**Diagram 5**

Turn the cover right side out. Remove the basting stitches from the ruffle. Insert the pillow form.

🧵 SEW SIMPLE

When gathering a ruffle, machine baste using water-soluble thread in the needle. Once the ruffle is gathered and permanently attached, press over the basting stitches with an iron and a damp press cloth. The needle thread will dissolve, and the bobbin thread will fall away.

NECK ROLL PILLOW

Size:

6½" (16.5cm) diameter × 16" (40.5cm) long
(excluding the ruffle)

SUPPLIES

- *⅜ yard (0.4m) of 45" to 54" (115cm to 138cm) wide decorator fabric, such as chintz, sateen, or polished cotton*
- *⅜ yard (0.4m) of 45" to 54" (115cm to 138cm) wide contrasting decorator fabric, such as chintz, sateen, or polished cotton*
- *2¼ yards (2.1m) of contrasting covered piping*
- *4 yards (3.7m) of 3½" (9cm) wide flat eyelet trim*
- *6½" × 16" (16.5cm × 40.5cm) neck roll pillow form*
- *1 sheet of typing paper*
- *Straight-edge ruler and pencil*

CUTTING DIRECTIONS

All measurements include ½" (1.3cm) seam allowances.

Fold the typing paper in half. Using the ruler, measure and mark a half circle with a 3¾" (9.5cm) radius, as shown in **Diagram 1.** Cut along the marked line.

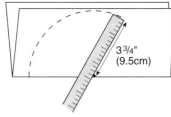

Diagram 1

3¾"
(9.5cm)

Unfold the paper and use it as a pattern for the 7½" (19cm) diameter ends of the neck roll.

From the decorator fabric, cut one 10¼" × 19¼" (26cm × 49cm) center panel.

From the contrasting decorator fabric, cut:

- *Two 4" × 19¼" (10cm × 49cm) side panels*
- *Two 7½" (19cm) diameter ends*

SEWING DIRECTIONS

1 Assembling the cover

On the right side of the center panel, machine baste the piping to the long edges, following the directions on page 126 for applying piping.

Referring to **Diagram 2,** with right sides together, stitch one side panel to each side edge of the center panel. Press the seam allowances toward the center panel.

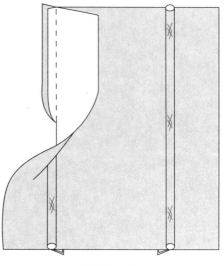

Diagram 2

With right sides together, fold the cover in half crosswise. Stitch, as shown in **Diagram 3,** leaving an opening large enough for turning the cover and inserting the pillow form.

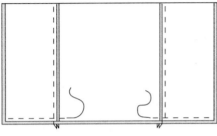

Diagram 3

2 Applying the piping and the ruffles

On the right side of the cover, machine baste the piping to the ends, following the directions on page 126 for applying piping.

Cut two pieces of eyelet, each 70" (178cm) long. With right sides together, stitch the ends of one piece of eyelet together, as shown in **Diagram 4.** Repeat for the other piece of eyelet. Press the seams open.

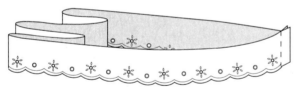

Diagram 4

🧵 SEW SIMPLE

When applying piping and ruffles to a pillow edge, make sure the ruffle is not caught in the permanent stitching. If necessary, rip out and restitch any problem areas.

Machine baste along the raw edge of each piece of eyelet, following the directions on page 125 for preparing a ruffle.

Divide and mark each eyelet ruffle into four sections.

Divide and mark each end of the cover into four sections.

Referring to **Diagram 5,** with right sides together, baste one ruffle to one end of the cover, following the directions on page 125 for gathering and attaching a ruffle. Using the sewing machine zipper foot attachment, baste through all of the layers, crowding the stitches close to the piping cord. Repeat for the other end of the cover.

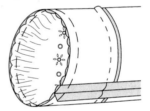

Diagram 5

3 Finishing the cover

Referring to **Diagram 6,** with right sides together, pin one end section to each end of the cover. Stitch the seams. Clip the curves.

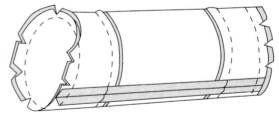

Diagram 6

Turn the cover right side out. Remove the basting stitches from the ruffle. Insert the pillow form. Slip stitch the opening closed, following the directions on page 125 for slip stitching.

COZY COMFORTER

Size:

To fit a standard twin-size, double, queen-size, or king-size bed

SUPPLIES

- *45" or 54" (115cm or 138cm) wide decorator fabric, such as chintz, sateen, or polished cotton**

- *45" (115cm) wide lining fabric, such as polished cotton or broadcloth**

- *1 sheet of polyester batting to equal the comforter's unfinished size**

- *Contrasting covered piping**

- *6" (15cm) wide ruffled eyelet trim**

- *Water-soluble marking pen*

*See the "Cutting Directions" for additional information.

SEW SIMPLE

If you can't find a sheet of batting that's large enough for your comforter, the batting can be pieced. To join two pieces of batting, butt the edges up against each other and sew them together by hand with a loose catch stitch, following the directions on page 125 for catch stitching.

CUTTING DIRECTIONS

All measurements include ½" (1.3cm) seam allowances.

Consult the chart below to determine how much fabric, lining, and trim (contrasting piping and ruffled eyelet) to purchase for your size mattress. Before purchasing fabric, review the information on page 124 for working with printed fabrics.

		COMFORTER				
		SIZE		YARDAGE		
	BED SIZE **(W × L)**	**UNFINISHED** **(W × L)**	**FINISHED** **(W × L)**	**FABRIC**	**LINING**	**TRIM**
Twin	39" × 75" (99cm × 191cm)	70" × 88" (178cm × 224cm)	69" × 87" (176cm × 221cm)	5 yards (4.6m)	5 yards (4.6m)	8½ yards (7.9m)
Double	54" × 75" (138cm × 191cm)	85" × 88" (216cm × 224cm)	84" × 87" (214cm × 221cm)	5 yards (4.6m)	5 yards (4.6m)	9¼ yards (8.5m)
Queen	60" × 80" (153cm × 204cm)	90" × 93" (229cm × 236cm)	89" × 92" (226cm × 234cm)	7¾ yards* (7.1m)	5¼ yards (4.9m)	10 yards (9.2m)
King	78" × 80" (199cm × 204cm)	108" × 93" (275cm × 236cm)	107" × 92" (272cm × 234cm)	7¾ yards (7.1m)	7¾ yards (7.1m)	11 yards (10.1m)

*For 45" (115cm) wide decorator fabric only; for 54" (138cm) wide decorator fabric, purchase 5¼ yards (4.9m).

Referring to **Diagram 1:**

- *From the decorator fabric, cut one front center panel and two front side panels in the length and width indicated for your mattress size.*

- *From the lining fabric, cut one lining center panel and two lining side panels in the length and width indicated for your mattress size.*

Cut the center panel from one full width of fabric. For a twin-size or double comforter, or for a queen-size comforter from 54″ (138cm) wide fabric, split the remaining fabric in half lengthwise and cut the side panels. For a queen-size comforter from 45″ (115cm) wide fabric or for a king-size comforter, cut each side panel from a full width of fabric.

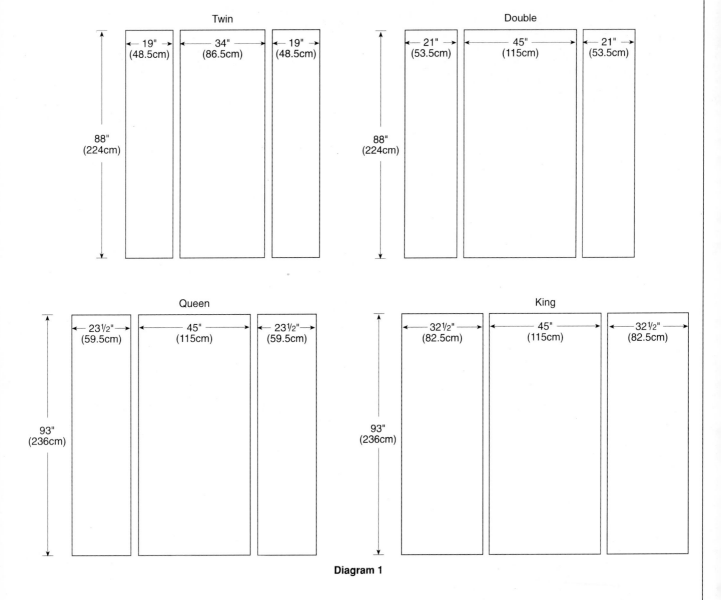

Diagram 1

SEWING DIRECTIONS

1 Preparing the front and the lining

With right sides together, stitch one front side panel to each side edge of the front center panel, as shown in **Diagram 2.** Press the seams open. Repeat for the lining panels.

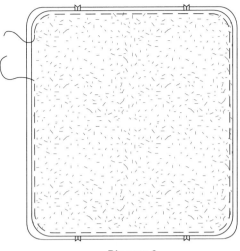

Diagram 3

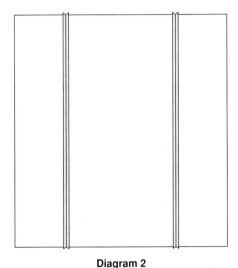

Diagram 2

Using a dinner plate as a template, round off all four corners of the comforter front. Repeat for the lining.

Pin the batting to the wrong side of the comforter front. Trim the batting to match the comforter. Machine baste the layers together ⅜" (1cm) from the raw edges, as shown in **Diagram 3.**

2 Applying the piping and the trim

On the right side of the comforter front, machine baste the piping in place around the edges, following the directions on page 126 for applying piping.

Referring to **Diagram 4,** with right sides together, pin the eyelet trim to the comforter front, over the piping. Unpin the trim at its cut ends. With right sides together, stitch the trim ends together so that the length of the circle of trim equals the circumference of the comforter. Finger press the seam open. Repin over the piping. Using the sewing machine zipper foot attachment, baste through all layers, crowding the stitches close to the piping cord.

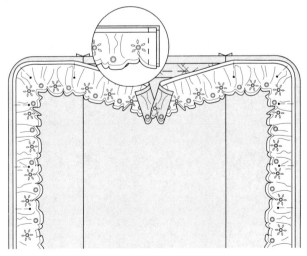

Diagram 4

3 Assembling the comforter

With right sides together, stitch the lining to the comforter front, leaving a 10″ (25.5cm) opening at one end, as shown in **Diagram 5.** Trim the corners on the diagonal and trim the batting close to the stitching.

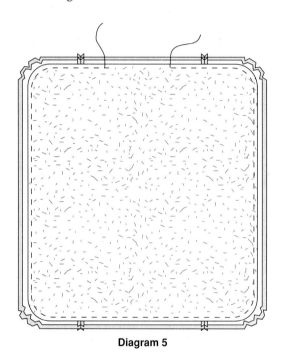

Diagram 5

Turn the comforter right side out. Slip stitch the opening closed, following the directions on page 125 for slip stitching.

4 Quilting the comforter

Referring to **Diagram 6,** use the marking pen to mark quilting lines on the comforter front. Pin the layers together every 4″ to 5″ (10cm to 12.5cm) along the quilting lines. Set the sewing machine stitch length for eight to ten stitches per inch (2.5cm). Machine stitch along the quilting lines, through all of the layers.

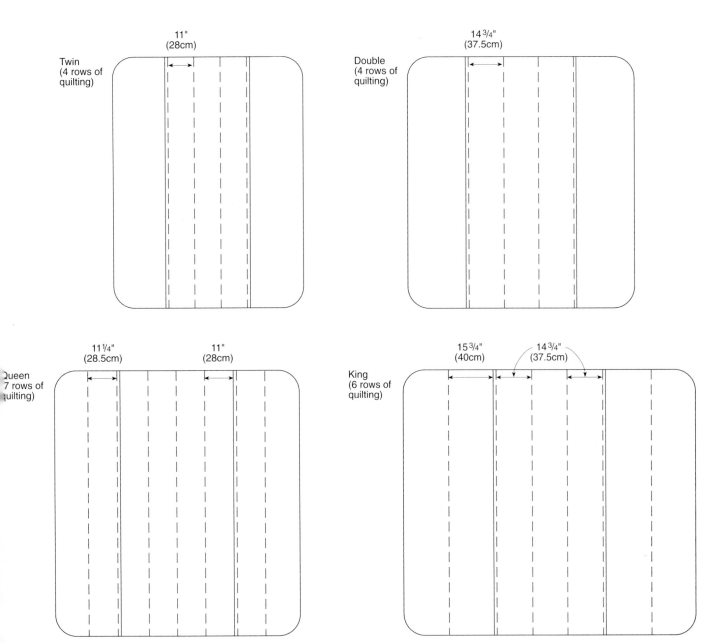

Diagram 6

GATHERED BED SKIRT

Size:

To fit a standard twin-size, double, queen-size, or king-size bed. The bed skirt measures 14" (35.5cm) long from the top of the box spring to the floor.

SUPPLIES

- *45" or 54" (115cm or 138cm) wide decorator fabric, such as chintz, sateen, or polished cotton**
- *1 fitted bedsheet to match the mattress size*
- *Dressmaker's chalk or a soft lead pencil*

*See the "Cutting Directions" for additional information.

CUTTING DIRECTIONS

All measurements include ½" (1.3cm) seam allowances.

The size of the bed determines how much fabric is required.

- *For a twin-size bed, purchase 4½ yards (4.2m).*
- *For a double bed, purchase 5 yards (4.6m).*
- *For a queen-size bed, purchase 5¼ yards (4.9m).*
- *For a king-size bed, purchase 6⅛ yards (5.7m).*

Before purchasing fabric, review the information on page 124 for working with printed fabrics.

From the decorator fabric, cut 15½" (39.5cm) long ruffle sections. Use the full width of the fabric as the width of each ruffle section.

- *For a twin-size bed, cut 10 ruffle sections.*
- *For a double bed, cut 11 ruffle sections.*
- *For a queen-size bed, cut 12 ruffle sections.*
- *For a king-size bed, cut 14 ruffle sections.*

SEWING DIRECTIONS

1 Marking the deck

Cover the box spring with the bedsheet. Using the dressmaker's chalk or a lead pencil, mark the edge of the box spring, as shown in **Diagram 1,** ending the line 3" (7.5cm) in from the corners at the head of the box spring. Divide and mark this line into eight equal parts.

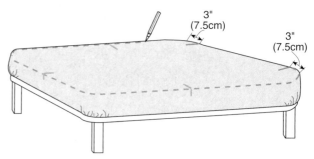

3"
(7.5cm)

3"
(7.5cm)

Diagram 1

Remove the bedsheet from the box spring.

🧵 SEW SIMPLE

Measure the distance from the top of your box spring to the floor (the drop). If it is more than 14" (35.5cm), you will need to purchase additional fabric and cut longer ruffle sections.

- *To determine the length of each ruffle section, add 1½" (3.8cm) to the drop measurement.*
- *To determine how many yards (meters) of fabric to purchase, multiply the ruffle length × 10 (for a twin-size bed), 11 (for a double bed), 12 (for a queen-size bed), or 14 (for a king-size bed). Divide this total by 36" (91.5cm).*

2 Assembling the ruffle

Referring to **Diagram 2,** with right sides together, stitch the ruffle sections together at the ends to form one long ruffle. Press the seams open. Press under 1″ (2.5cm) on one long edge. Tuck the raw edge in to meet the crease. Press again. Stitch close to the second fold.

Press under ½″ (1.3cm) on each side of the ruffle. Tuck the raw edge in to meet the crease. Press again. Stitch close to the second fold.

Machine baste along the raw edge, following the directions on page 125 for preparing a ruffle.

3 Attaching the ruffle

Divide and mark the ruffle into eight equal parts.

Referring to **Diagram 3,** with right sides together, stitch the ruffle to the fitted sheet, matching the ruffle seam line to the marked line on the sheet and following the directions on page 125 for gathering and attaching a ruffle.

Press the ruffle and ruffle seam allowance down, away from the top of the sheet.

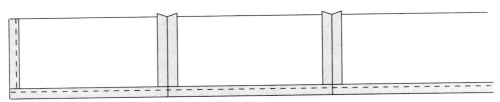

Diagram 2

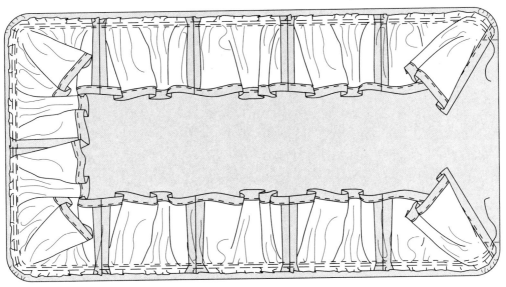

Diagram 3

Crisp edges and simple shapes give a mock-pleated bed skirt and buttoned duvet cover, plus flanged pillow shams and covers, their timeless appeal.

TAILORED TO PERFECTION

FLANGED PILLOW SHAM

Size:

20″ × 26″ (51cm × 66cm) (excluding the flange)

SUPPLIES

- *1½ yards (1.4m) of 45″, 54″, or 60″ (115cm, 138cm, or 153cm) wide decorator fabric, such as chintz, sateen, or polished cotton*
- *¾ yard (0.7m) of polyester batting*
- *One 20″ × 26″ (51cm × 66cm) standard-size bed pillow*
- *Water-soluble marking pen*

CUTTING DIRECTIONS

All measurements include ½″ (1.3cm) seam allowances.

From the decorator fabric, cut:

- *One 25″ × 31″ (63.5cm × 78.5cm) sham front*
- *Two 21″ × 25″ (53.5cm × 63.5cm) sham backs*

From the batting, cut one 25″ × 31″ (63.5cm × 78.5cm) rectangle.

SEWING DIRECTIONS

1 Preparing the front

Pin the batting rectangle to the wrong side of the sham front. Machine baste the layers together ⅜″ (1cm) from the raw edges, as shown in **Diagram 1.**

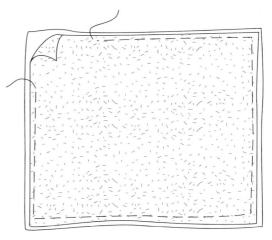

Diagram 1

🧵 SEW SIMPLE

If the batting shifts during machine basting, reduce the pressure on the sewing machine's presser foot.

⊕ DESIGN PLUS

Instead of straight stitching, use contrasting thread and a decorative machine embroidery stitch along the marked rectangle.

2 Preparing the back

Referring to **Diagram 2,** press under ¼″ (6mm) on one short end of one sham back. Press under again 1½″ (3.8cm). Stitch close to the first fold. Repeat for the other sham back.

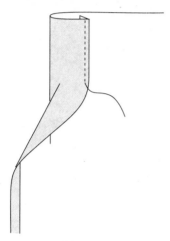

Diagram 2

3 Finishing the sham

Referring to **Diagram 3,** with right sides together, pin the sham backs to the sham front so that the back finished edges overlap. Stitch ½″ (1.3cm) from the cut edge, all around the cover. Trim the corners on the diagonal and trim the seam allowances to ¼″ (6mm).

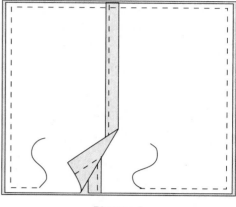

Diagram 3

Turn the sham right side out. Press. Referring to **Diagram 4,** use the marking pen to mark 2″ (5cm) in from each edge, drawing a rectangle. Stitch around the marked rectangle through all of the layers, creating the flange. Insert the pillow.

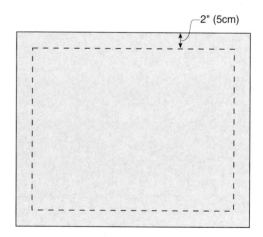

2″ (5cm)

Diagram 4

FLANGED PILLOW COVER

Size:

12" (30.5cm) square (excluding the flange)

SUPPLIES

- *½ yard (0.5m) of 45", 54", or 60" (115cm, 138cm, or 153cm) wide decorator fabric, such as chintz, sateen, or polished cotton*
- *½ yard (0.5m) of polyester batting*
- *One 12" (30.5cm) square pillow form*
- *Water-soluble marking pen*

CUTTING DIRECTIONS

All measurements include ½" (1.3cm) seam allowances.

From the decorator fabric, cut:

- *One 17" (43cm) square cover front*
- *Two 13¼" × 17" (33.5cm × 43cm) cover backs*

From the batting, cut one 17" (43cm) square.

🧵 SEW SIMPLE

For faster sewing, eliminate the cover back hems. Purchase 1 yard (1m) of fabric and increase the size of both cover backs to 17" × 23" (43cm × 58.5cm). Fold each cover back in half with wrong sides together and the 17" (43cm) edges matching. Use the folded edges as the back finished edges.

SEWING DIRECTIONS

1 Preparing the front

Pin the batting square to the wrong side of the cover front. Machine baste the layers together ⅜" (1cm) from the raw edges, as shown in **Diagram 1.**

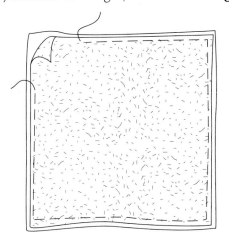

Diagram 1

2 Preparing the back

Referring to **Diagram 2,** press under ¼" (6mm) on one short end of one cover back. Press under again 1½" (3.8cm). Stitch close to the first fold. Repeat for the other cover back.

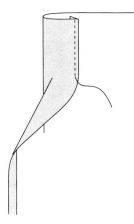

Diagram 2

3 Finishing the cover

Referring to **Diagram 3,** with right sides together, pin the cover backs to the cover front so that the back finished edges overlap. Stitch ½" (1.3cm) from the cut edge, all around the cover. Trim the corners on the diagonal and trim the seam allowances to ¼" (6mm).

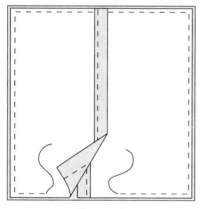

Diagram 3

Turn the cover right side out. Press. Referring to **Diagram 4,** use the marking pen to mark 2" (5cm) in from each edge, drawing a square. Stitch around the marked square through all of the layers, creating the flange. Insert the pillow form.

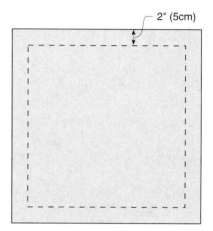

Diagram 4

⊕ DESIGN PLUS

To add textural interest to the pillow, machine quilt the flange. Mark and stitch squares ½", 1", and 1½" (1.3cm, 2.5cm, and 3.8cm) in from the edge of the pillow.

DUVET COVER

Size:

To fit a standard twin-size, double, queen-size, or king-size comforter or duvet

SUPPLIES

- *45" or 54" (115cm or 138cm) wide decorator fabric, such as chintz, sateen, or polished cotton**
- *45" or 54" (115cm or 138cm) wide contrasting decorator fabric**
- *3/4" (2cm) diameter buttons: 2 for a twin-size; 4 for a double or queen-size; 5 for a king-size comforter*
- *Purchased comforter or duvet*
- *Water-soluble marking pen*

*See the "Cutting Directions" for additional information.

CUTTING DIRECTIONS

All measurements include ½" (1.3cm) seam allowances.

Measure the length and width of your comforter or duvet. Consult the chart below to determine how much fabric and contrasting fabric to purchase for your size comforter or duvet. If your comforter or duvet is longer than the one listed for your size bed, consult the "Design Plus" tip on page 31 before purchasing fabric. In addition, before purchasing fabric, review the information on page 124 for working with printed fabrics.

Referring to **Diagram 1** on page 30:

- *From the decorator fabric, cut one front center panel and two front side panels in the length and width indicated for your comforter or duvet size.*
- *From the contrasting fabric, cut one back center panel and two back side panels in the length and width indicated for your comforter or duvet size.*

		DUVET COVER		
		PURCHASED COMFORTER/DUVET (W × L)	YARDAGE	
	BED SIZE (W × L)		DECORATOR FABRIC	CONTRASTING FABRIC
Twin	39" × 75" (99cm × 191cm)	68" × 86" (173cm × 219cm)	5⅛ yards (4.7m)	6¼ yards (5.8m)
Double	54" × 75" (138cm × 191cm)	86" × 86" (219cm × 219cm)	5⅛ yards (4.7m)	6¼ yards (5.8m)
Queen	60" × 80" (153cm × 204cm)	86" × 86" (219cm × 219cm)	7⅝ yards* (7m)	9¾ yards* (9m)
King	78" × 80" (199cm × 204cm)	101" × 90" (257cm × 229cm)	7⅝ yards (7m)	9¾ yards (9m)

*For 45" (115cm) wide decorator fabric only; for 54" (138cm) wide decorator fabric, purchase 5⅛ yards (4.7m) of decorator fabric and 6¼ yards (5.8m) of contrasting fabric.

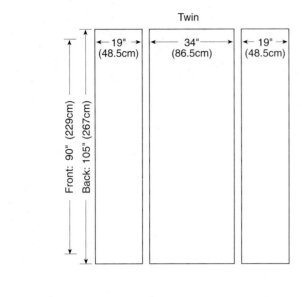

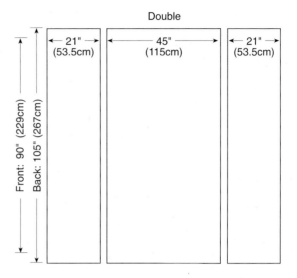

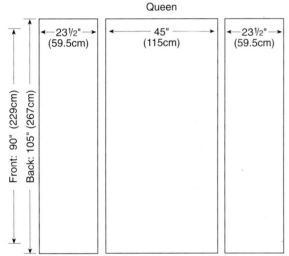

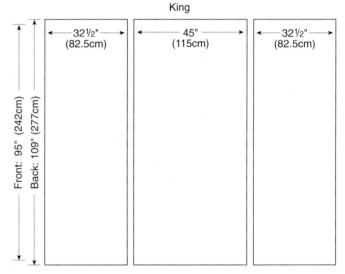

Diagram 1

Cut the center panels from one full width of fabric. For a twin-size or double cover, or for a queen-size cover from 54" (138cm) wide fabric, split the remaining fabric in half lengthwise and cut the side panels. For a queen-size cover from 45" (115cm) fabric or for a king-size cover, cut each side panel from a full width of fabric.

🧵 SEW SIMPLE

A few fabrics are available in 120" (305cm) widths, eliminating the need for side panels and piecing seams. Purchase enough decorator fabric to cut a front panel equal to the comforter or duvet length plus 4" (10cm). Purchase enough contrasting fabric to cut a back panel equal to the comforter or duvet length plus 19" (48.5cm). Cut each panel to equal the width of the comforter or duvet plus 2" (5cm).

SEWING DIRECTIONS

1 Preparing the front

Referring to **Diagram 2,** with right sides together, stitch one front side panel to each side edge of the front center panel. Press the seams open.

Press under 2″ (5cm) on the upper edge of the front. Press the raw edge under ¼″ (6mm). Stitch close to the second fold.

2 Preparing the back

Referring to **Diagram 3,** with right sides together, stitch one back side panel to each side edge of the back center panel. Press the seams open.

Press under 4½″ (11.5cm) on the upper edge of the back. Press the raw edge under ¼″ (6mm). Stitch close to the second fold.

⊕ DESIGN PLUS

Commercial comforters and duvets do not all conform to the same measurements. Here's what to do if your comforter's or duvet's measurements do not match the ones in the chart on page 29.

- *If your comforter or duvet is wider or narrower, divide the difference in half. Adjust the cutting width of the front and back side panels by this amount.*

- *If your comforter or duvet is shorter, subtract the difference from the cutting length of all of the panels.*

- *If your comforter or duvet is longer, add the difference to the cutting length of all of the panels. In order to do this, you'll need to purchase extra decorator fabric and contrasting fabric. For a twin-size or double cover, or for a queen-size cover from 54″ (138cm) wide fabric, add two times the extra length to the yardage requirements in the chart on page 29. For a queen-size cover from 45″ (115cm) wide fabric or for a king-size cover, add three times the extra length to the yardage requirements.*

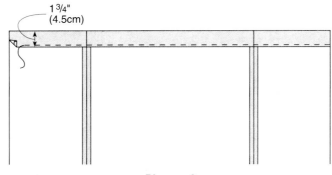

1 3/4″ (4.5cm)

Diagram 2

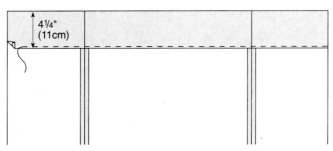

4¼″ (11cm)

Diagram 3

Referring to **Diagram 4,** use the marking pen to mark the buttonhole placement. Place the marks at evenly spaced intervals, 2″ (5cm) from the upper edge of the back. For the twin-size, make two marks; for the double and the queen-size, make four marks; for the king-size, make five marks. Measure down 12″ (30.5cm) from the upper edge along each side and mark for the overlap fold line.

Make one machine buttonhole at each buttonhole marking. Stitch the buttonholes so that they are parallel to the side edges.

3 Assembling the cover

Fold the upper edge of the back to the right side along the overlap fold line; pin.

With right sides together and raw edges even, pin the front to the back at the sides and lower edges. Stitch, as shown in **Diagram 5.**

Press the seams open. Turn the cover right side out. Press the cover flat. Hand sew the buttons in place on the cover front to correspond to the buttonholes.

Insert the comforter or duvet into the cover. Button the cover closed.

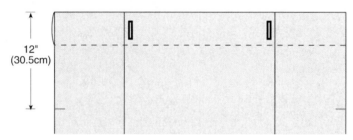

12″
(30.5cm)

Diagram 4

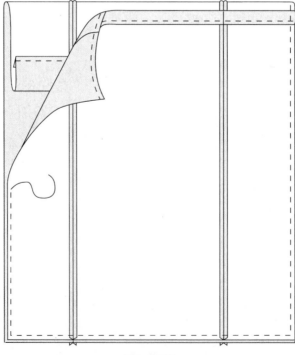

Diagram 5

TAILORED BED SKIRT

Size:

To fit a standard twin-size, double, queen-size, or king-size bed. The bed skirt measures 14″ (35.5cm) long from the top of the box spring to the floor.

SUPPLIES

- *54″ (138cm) wide decorator fabric, such as chintz, sateen, or polished cotton**
- *1 fitted bedsheet to match the mattress size*
- *Water-soluble marking pen*

*See the "Cutting Directions" for additional information.

CUTTING DIRECTIONS

All measurements include ½″ (1.3cm) seam allowances.

The size of the bed determines how much fabric is required:

- *For a twin-size bed, purchase 2⅜ yards (2.2m).*
- *For a double, queen-size, or king-size bed, purchase 2¾ yards (2.6m).*

Before purchasing fabric, review the information on page 124 for working with printed fabrics.

From the decorator fabric, cut 15½″ (39.5cm) long skirt sections. Use the full width of the fabric as the width of each skirt section.

- *For a twin-size bed, cut five skirt sections.*
- *For a double, queen-size, or king-size bed, cut six skirt sections.*

SEWING DIRECTIONS

1   Marking the deck

Cover the box spring with the bedsheet. Using the marking pen, mark the edge of the box spring, as shown in **Diagram 1,** ending the line 3″ (7.5cm) in from the corners at the head of the box spring. Mark each side center between the top and bottom edge of the box spring. Mark the bottom edge center between the two side edges.

Remove the bedsheet from the box spring.

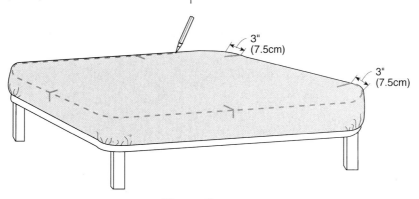

3″
(7.5cm)

3″
(7.5cm)

Diagram 1

SEW SIMPLE

Measure the distance from the top of your box spring to the floor (the drop). If it is more than 14" (35.5cm), you will need to purchase additional fabric and cut longer skirt sections.

- *To determine the length of each skirt section, add 1½" (3.8cm) to the drop measurement.*
- *To determine how many yards (meters) of fabric to purchase, multiply the skirt length × 5 (for a twin-size bed) or × 6 (for a double, queen-size, or king-size bed). Divide this total by 36" (91.5cm).*

2 Preparing the side panels

- *For a twin-size or a double bed, stitch three full skirt sections together at the ends to form one long section. Press the seams open. Cut the section into two side panels that each measure 80" (204cm) wide × 15½" (39.5cm) long.*
- *For a queen-size or king-size bed, stitch four full skirt sections together at the ends to form one long section. Press the seams open. Cut the section into two side panels that each measure 85" (216cm) wide × 15½" (39.5cm) long.*

On one side panel, mark 3½" (9cm) from one end. Fold the panel so that the other end matches the mark, as shown in **Diagram 2.** Cut along the fold. Using the marking pen, label the longer panel "A" and the shorter panel "B." Repeat for the other side panel.

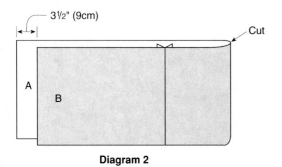

Diagram 2

3 Preparing the bottom panels and the underlays

- *For a twin-size bed, cut two 20½" (52cm) wide × 15½" (39.5cm) long bottom panels from one skirt section.*
- *For a double bed, cut two 28" (71cm) wide × 15½" (39.5cm) long bottom panels. Cut each panel from a different skirt section.*
- *For a queen-size bed, cut two 31" (78.5cm) wide × 15½" (39.5cm) long bottom panels. Cut each panel from a different skirt section.*
- *For a king-size bed, cut two 40" (102cm) wide × 15½" (39.5cm) long bottom panels. Cut each panel from a different skirt section.*

Using the marking pen, label each bottom panel "C."

From the remaining full and partial skirt sections, cut five 12" (30.5cm) wide × 15½" (39.5cm) long underlays.

4 Hemming the panels and the underlays

Referring to **Diagram 3,** press under 1" (2.5cm) on one long edge of one side panel. Tuck the raw edge in to meet the crease. Press again. Stitch close to the second fold. Repeat, hemming one long edge of each panel and one 12" (30.5cm) edge of each underlay.

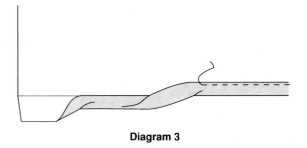

Diagram 3

Press under ½" (1.3cm) on each side of one side panel. Tuck the raw edge in to meet the crease. Press again. Stitch close to the second fold. Repeat, hemming both sides of all of the panels and underlays.

5 Assembling the bed skirt

Referring to **Diagram 4,** with right sides together, pin the panels to the bedsheet, matching the seam line on the panels to the marked line on the bedsheet. Position the panels so that panels A and B just meet at the side center mark, panels B and C just meet at the bottom corners, and the two C panels meet at the bottom center mark. Make a ⅜″ (1cm) long clip in the panel A seam allowances at the corner marks. If necessary, make additional clips on each side of the marks until the fabric turns smoothly around the corners. Machine baste along the seam line.

Fold each underlay in half, side edges matching. Mark the center at the upper edge.

Referring to **Diagram 5,** pin one underlay, right side down, over the two C panels, matching the raw edges and the center mark on the underlay to the point where the C panels meet. Repeat, pinning one underlay at each bottom corner and each side

center. Make ⅜″ (1cm) long clips in the underlay seam allowances at the bottom corner marks. If necessary, make additional clips on each side of the marks until the fabric turns smoothly around the bottom corners. Stitch ½″ (1.3cm) from the raw edges of the panels through all of the layers.

Press the panels and the panel seam allowances down, away from the top of the bedsheet.

⊕ DESIGN PLUS

Use 1½″ (39mm) wide grosgrain ribbon to add a contrasting band to the lower edge of this bed skirt. To apply the ribbon and hem the panels in one easy step, press the lower edge of each panel up 1″ (2.5cm) to the right side. Using a glue stick, baste the ribbon in place over the hem allowance, matching the lower edge of the ribbon to the folded edge of the panel. Stitch the ribbon along both long edges.

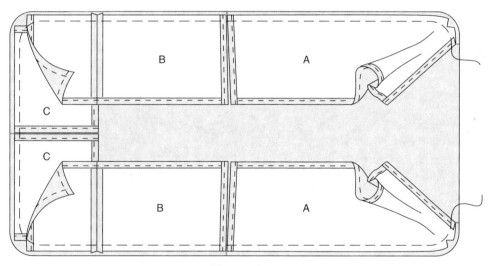

Diagram 4

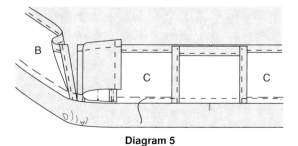

Diagram 5

A draped canopy, envelope-style duvet cover, and piles of pillows are all cleverly fashioned from easy-care sheets and pillowcases.

RIBBON-TIED PILLOW

Size:

20″ × 26″ (51cm × 66cm)

SUPPLIES

- *1 flat or fitted twin-size sheet*
- *8 yards (7.4m) of ⅞″ (23mm) wide ribbon*
- *One 20″ × 26″ (51cm × 66cm) standard-size bed pillow*
- *Water-soluble marking pen*

CUTTING DIRECTIONS

All measurements include ½″ (1.3cm) seam allowances.

From the twin-size sheet, cut two 27″ × 41″ (68.5cm × 104cm) rectangles.

From the ribbon, cut twenty 14″ (35.5cm) long ties. If desired, notch one end of each tie.

SEWING DIRECTIONS

1   Attaching the ties

Fold one rectangle in half with the 27″ (68.5cm) sides matching.

Press, making a crease at the fold. Unfold the rectangle.

Working on the right side of the rectangle, measure and mark with the marking pen along one short edge, 1″ (2.5cm) from each corner. Make two more marks, evenly spaced in between. Repeat for the other short edge. Measure and mark one long edge ½″ (1.3cm) to the right and left of the crease. Make two more marks on each side of the crease, spacing the marks 6½″ (16.5cm) apart. Repeat for the other long edge. Center and pin one tie at each mark, as shown in **Diagram 1.**

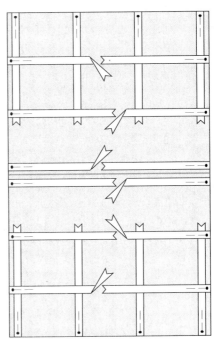

Diagram 1

⊕ DESIGN PLUS

This pretty tie-on cover is a great way to spruce up a faded toss pillow. The old cover will peek out at the edges, creating an attractive two-tone effect.

2 Assembling the cover

With right sides together, pin the two rectangles together.

Stitch, leaving an opening along one side edge large enough for turning. Trim the corners, as shown in **Diagram 2.**

Diagram 2

Turn the rectangle right side out. Press. Slip stitch the opening closed, following the directions on page 125 for slip stitching.

3 Securing the cover

Place the pillow on one half of the cover. Fold the other half of the cover over the pillow and tie the corresponding ribbons together in bows, as shown in **Diagram 3** and following the directions on page 128 for tying a bow.

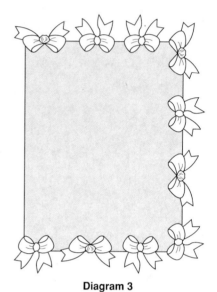

Diagram 3

🧵 SEW SIMPLE

It's easy to adapt this cover to any size pillow. Adjust the size of each rectangle to equal the width of the pillow plus 1" (2.5cm) × twice the length of the pillow plus 1" (2.5cm). If the pillow is smaller than 16" (40.5cm) square, purchase 5½ yards (5.1m) of ribbon. Cut the ribbon into fourteen 14" (35.5cm) long ties.

QUICK-FOLD PILLOW

Size:

20″ (51cm) square

SUPPLIES

- One 20″ × 30″ (51cm × 76cm) standard-size pillowcase with a decorative hem
- Three 1¼″ (3.2cm) diameter buttons or 3 yards (2.8m) of 1½″ (39mm) wide ribbon
- One 20″ (51cm) square pillow form
- Water-soluble marking pen

SEWING DIRECTIONS

1 Marking the pillowcase

Working on one side of the pillowcase and using the marking pen, divide and mark the hem edge into four equal parts, as shown in **Diagram 1.**

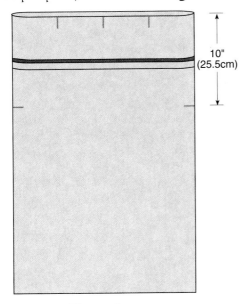

10″
(25.5cm)

Diagram 1

Measure down 10″ (25.5cm) from the hem edge along both sides of the pillowcase and mark for a fold line.

2 Making the closures

For the buttoned version:

Referring to **Diagram 2,** make three machine buttonholes, aligning them with the hem edge markings and stitching through only one layer of the pillowcase. Position each buttonhole so it is centered in the hem area and perpendicular to the hemmed edge. Make three corresponding buttonholes on the other side of the pillowcase.

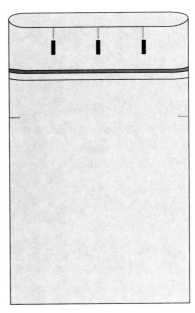

Diagram 2

⊕ DESIGN PLUS

Dye lots vary and sheet patterns may be discontinued at any time. If you are planning several projects for the same room, make sure you purchase all of the sheets at the same time to avoid future disappointment.

Fold the pillowcase down along the fold line and mark for the button placement. Sew one button at each marking, sewing through only one layer of the pillowcase, as shown in **Diagram 3.**

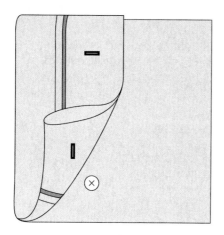

Diagram 3

For the tied version:

Cut the ribbon into six 18″ (45.5cm) long ties.

Fold the pillowcase down along the fold line. Referring to **Diagram 4,** measure up 10″ (25.5cm) from the bottom edge and mark to correspond to the hem edge markings. On the inside of the pillowcase, pin one tie at each of the hem edge marks. On the outside of the pillowcase, pin one tie at each of the remaining marks. Stitch the ties in place, stitching through only one layer of the pillowcase.

3 **Securing the cover**

Insert the pillow form into the pillowcase. Fold down the top of the pillowcase and button the buttons or tie the ribbons into bows, as shown in the photograph on page 36 and following the directions on page 128 for tying a bow.

🧵 SEW SIMPLE

To keep the ribbon ties from fraying, seal the cut ends with a liquid ravel preventer, such as Fray Check.

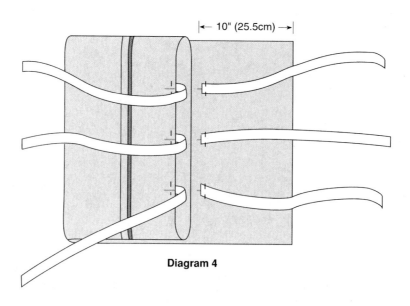

Diagram 4

EASY NECK ROLL PILLOW

Size:

14" (35.5cm) long (excluding the ends)

SUPPLIES

- *One 20" × 30" (51cm × 76cm) standard-size pillowcase*
- *1 yard (1m) of ⅞" (23mm) wide ribbon*
- *One 6" × 14" (15cm × 35.5cm) neck roll pillow form*
- *Seam ripper or small scissors*

CUTTING DIRECTIONS

All measurements include ½" (1.3cm) seam allowances.

Using the seam ripper or small scissors, rip out the pillowcase seam. Press the pillowcase flat. From the pillowcase, cut one 21" × 40" (53.5cm × 102cm) rectangle.

SEWING DIRECTIONS

1 Assembling the cover

With right sides together, stitch the two long edges of the rectangle together, as shown in **Diagram 1.** Press the seam open.

Diagram 1

✇ SEW SIMPLE

Use rubber bands to secure the ends of the neck roll. Tie the ribbon in place over the rubber bands.

2 Hemming the cover

Fold one raw edge up ½" (1.3cm) and press. Fold it up 6" (15cm) and press again. Machine stitch close to the first fold, as shown in **Diagram 2.** Repeat for the other raw edge.

Diagram 2

3 Securing the cover

Cut the ribbon into two 18" (45.5cm) long pieces.

Turn the cover right side out. Insert the pillow form. Tie the ends closed with the ribbon, as shown in the photograph on page 36, and following the directions on page 128 for tying a bow.

⚙ DESIGN PLUS

To embellish the edges of the cover, purchase 1¼ yards (1.2m) of jumbo rickrack or ⅞" (23mm) wide ribbon. Stitch or fuse the ribbon or rickrack in place around the outer edge of the hem.

ENVELOPE DUVET COVER

Size:

To fit a standard twin-size, full-size, queen-size, or king-size duvet or comforter

SUPPLIES

- *2 flat sheets**
- *2 yards (1.9m) of twill tape or ½" (12mm) wide ribbon*
- *1" (2.5cm) diameter buttons: 9 for a twin-size, 11 for a full- or queen-size, or 15 for a king-size cover*
- *Purchased duvet or comforter*
- *Water-soluble marking pen*

*See the "Cutting Directions" for additional information.

CUTTING DIRECTIONS

All measurements include ½" (1.3cm) seam allowances.

The size of the purchased duvet or comforter determines the size of the two flat sheets.

- *For a twin-size duvet or comforter, purchase two full-size sheets.*
- *For a full- or queen-size duvet or comforter, purchase two queen-size sheets.*
- *For a king-size duvet or comforter, purchase two king-size sheets.*

For the cover back, choose a solid color sheet (which looks the same on both sides) or a printed sheet with a decorative border that is at least 5" (12.5cm) deep.

For the cover front, choose any coordinating flat sheet.

Purchased duvets and comforters are not all exactly the same size. Measure your duvet or comforter before cutting the cover sections.

From the coordinating sheet, cut one cover front equal to the width of the duvet or comforter plus 1" (2.5cm) × the length of the duvet or comforter plus 2½" (6.3cm). Begin measuring the length from the lower edge of the sheet and cut off the excess at the top.

From one solid color sheet or a sheet with a decorative hem, cut one cover back equal to the width of the duvet or comforter plus 1" (2.5cm) × the length of the duvet or comforter plus ½" (1.3cm) plus the depth of the decorative hem or 5" (12.5cm). Begin measuring the length from the upper edge of the sheet and cut off the excess at the bottom.

SEWING DIRECTIONS

1 **Hemming the cover front**

Press under 1" (2.5cm) along the upper edge of the cover top and then 1" (2.5cm) again. Stitch close to the first fold, as shown in **Diagram 1.**

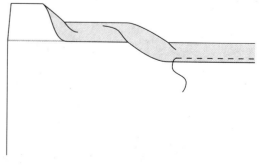

Diagram 1

⊕ DESIGN PLUS

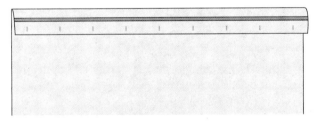

For a warm and cozy winter cover, choose flannel sheets.

2 Preparing the cover back

Place the cover back right side up. Fold the upper edge down 5″ (12.5cm) or the full amount of the decorative hem to form the flap. Press.

Referring to **Diagram 2,** use the marking pen to mark the buttonhole placement across the flap.

Diagram 2

Mark the first buttonhole at the center and then evenly space the remaining buttonholes between the center and each side. Make 9 marks for a twin-size, 11 for a full- or queen-size, or 15 for a king-size duvet or comforter.

Unfold the sheet. Make one machine buttonhole at each buttonhole marking. Stitch the buttonholes so they are parallel to the side edges.

3 Assembling the cover

With right sides together and referring to **Diagram 3,** pin the cover front to the cover back. Stitch along the side and lower edges.

Cut the twill tape or ribbon into eight 9″ (23cm) long ties. Stitch one tie to the seam allowances at each corner of the cover, as shown in **Diagram 4.**

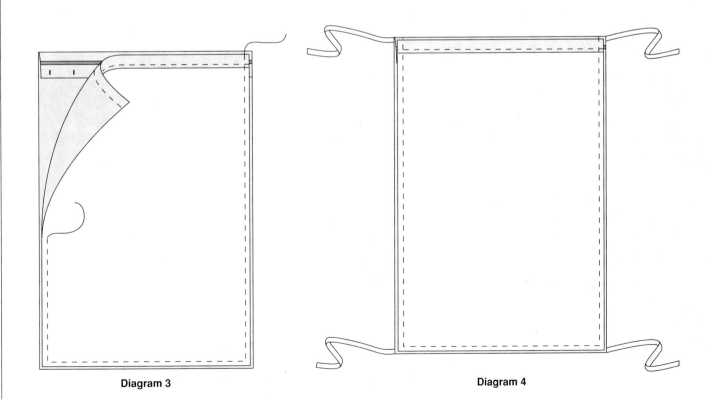

Diagram 3

Diagram 4

Press the side and lower seam allowances open. Turn the cover right side out. Press the side and lower edges flat. Turn the flap right side out over the cover front, as shown in **Diagram 5.**

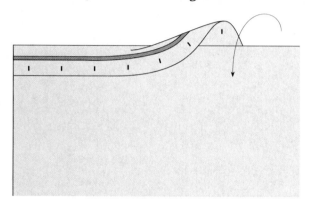

Diagram 5

Hand sew the buttons in place on the cover front to correspond to the buttonholes, as shown in **Diagram 6.**

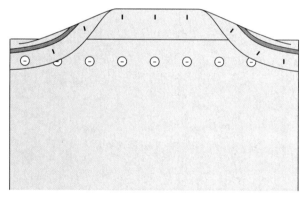

Diagram 6

SEW SIMPLE

To sew the buttons on fast, double the thread and then thread the needle. Using four thicknesses of thread, instead of the usual two, means you only have to make half as many passes with the needle.

4 **Securing the cover**

Hand sew one tie to each corner on the outside of the duvet or comforter.

Turn the cover wrong side out. Place the duvet or comforter on top of the cover. Tie the corresponding tapes or ribbons together. Reach inside the cover and grab the bottom corners. Pull them out through the opening, turning the cover right side out in the process. Shake to distribute the duvet or comforter in the cover.

DRAPED CANOPY

Size:

To fit a standard twin-size, double, queen-size, or king-size bed

SUPPLIES

- *Flat sheets**
- *Three 8" (20.5cm) diameter grapevine wreaths*
- *Floral materials to coordinate with your sheets (here, we used silk roses, silk ivy leaves, dried baby's-breath, and dried German statice)*
- *Seam ripper or small scissors*
- *Hot-glue gun and glue sticks*
- *18-gauge wire*
- *3 nails or hooks to hang the wreaths*
- *T-pins*

*See the "Cutting Directions" for additional information.

CUTTING DIRECTIONS

All measurements include ½" (1.3cm) seam allowances.

The size of the bed determines the size of the flat sheets.

- *For a twin-size bed, purchase two full-size sheets.*
- *For a double bed, purchase two queen-size sheets.*
- *For a queen-size bed, purchase two king-size sheets.*
- *For a king-size bed, purchase three king-size sheets.*

Using a seam ripper or small scissors, rip out the hems at the sides and lower edges of all of the sheets.

For a king-size bed only, rip out the hem and/or cut off any decorative trim or border at the upper edge of one sheet.

Press the edges of all of the sheets.

SEWING DIRECTIONS

1 Assembling the canopy

For a twin-size, double, or queen-size bed, with right sides together and referring to **Diagram 1,** pin the two sheets together at the lower edges and stitch. Press the seam open.

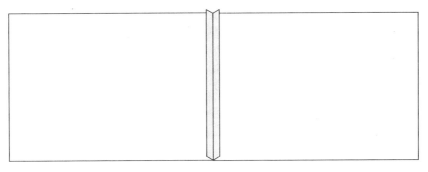

Diagram 1

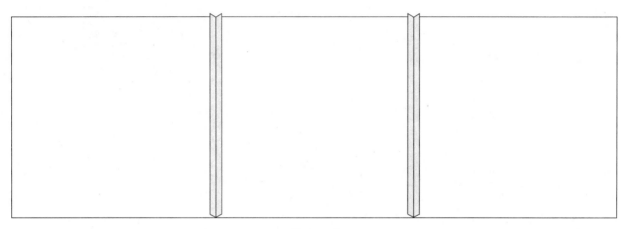

Diagram 2

For a king-size bed, with right sides together and referring to **Diagram 2,** pin the lower edge of one sheet to the upper edge of the sheet with the upper hem or border removed. Stitch. With right sides together, pin the lower edge of the third sheet to the lower edge of the sheet with the upper hem or border removed. Stitch. Press both seams open.

For all size beds, with right sides together, fold the sheets in half lengthwise. Pin and stitch, as shown in **Diagram 3.** Turn the sheets right side out and press.

2 Decorating the wreaths

Glue some of the roses and ivy leaves in place on one wreath. Shape the petals and leaves to give them a natural look.

Cut some statice and baby's-breath into small pieces. Glue them onto the wreath, filling in the spaces between the roses and ivy leaves.

Decorate the remaining wreaths to match the first.

Use the wire to make a secure loop on the back of each wreath.

3 Mounting the wreaths

Install the hooks or nails on the wall above the bed. Position one hook or nail so that it is centered over the bed, approximately 72″ (183cm) from the floor. Position the other two hooks or nails so that one aligns with each corner of the bed and both are approximately 60″ (153cm) from the floor, as shown in the photograph on page 36.

Hang the wreaths on the hooks or nails.

> ### SEW SIMPLE
>
> *Sheets have a protective sizing that repels stains and dirt. To keep your canopy looking fresh, do not launder it. Instead, vacuum it periodically.*

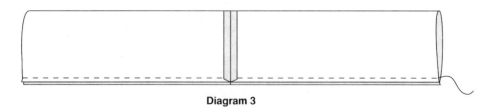

Diagram 3

4 Hanging the canopy

Lay the canopy out on the floor or other large, flat surface. Smooth it out. Starting at the long, folded edge, fold the fabric lengthwise into 4" to 6" (10cm to 15cm) deep accordion pleats, as shown in **Diagram 4.** Use T-pins to temporarily secure the pleats. For the king-size canopy, use T-pins to temporarily mark the center of the canopy.

Referring to the photograph on page 36, drape the canopy through the wreaths. Match the center seam or the center T-pins to the center wreath. Use T-pins to secure the back of the canopy to the back of the center wreath. Adjust the canopy so that it drapes evenly on both sides of the center wreath. Remove the temporary T-pins and gently pull the pleats apart. Use T-pins to secure the canopy to the back of the side wreaths.

⊕ DESIGN PLUS

To make the coordinated bed skirt in the photograph on page 36, you will need one flat sheet for the skirt and one fitted bedsheet for the deck. Both sheets should be the same size as your mattress. Follow the directions on page 22 for the Gathered Bed Skirt, cutting the flat sheet into six 15½" (39.5cm) long ruffle sections. Use the full width of the sheet as the width of each ruffle section. If desired, add ribbon or flat trim to the lower edge of the bed skirt.

Diagram 4

Two *full-size sheets and simple no-sew techniques are the magic ingredients to spruce up a bathroom sink or dress up a bedroom vanity.*

VANITY FAIR

Size:

To fit a dressing table with an approximately 60″ (153cm) circumference

SUPPLIES

- *2 full-size flat sheets with decorative hems*
- *4-cord smocking tape with built-in plush loops, such as Gosling Tapes Sew Easy quick-hold smocking tape**
- *2″ (5cm) wide adhesive-backed hook tape, such as Gosling Tapes Sew Easy quick-hold peel and stick hook tape**

*See the "Cutting Directions" for additional information.

CUTTING DIRECTIONS

All measurements include ½″ (1.3cm) seam allowances.

Referring to **Diagram 1,** measure around the outer edge of the table for the finished circumference of the skirt (A). Measure from the edge of the table to the floor for the finished length of the skirt (B).

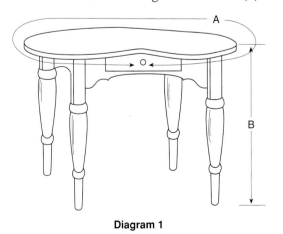

Diagram 1

Purchase enough smocking tape to equal two and a half times the finished circumference (A).

Purchase enough adhesive-backed hook tape to equal the finished circumference (A).

Referring to **Diagram 2,** from one flat sheet, cut one skirt panel, using the edge of the decorative hem as the lower edge of the panel. For the cutting length, add 1″ (2.5cm) to the finished length (B). For the cutting width, multiply the finished circumference (A) by 1.25 and then add 2″ (5cm). Repeat, cutting another panel from the other flat sheet.

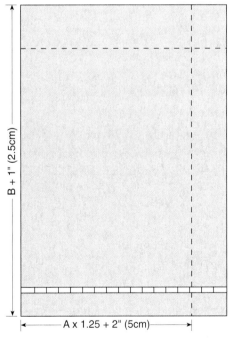

Diagram 2

SEWING DIRECTIONS

1 Hemming the panels

Press under 1″ (2.5cm) on one side edge of one panel. Tuck the raw edge in to meet the crease. Press again. Stitch close to the second fold, as shown in **Diagram 3.** Repeat for the other side edge. Then repeat for the other panel.

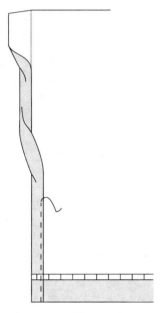

Diagram 3

2 Making the headers

Cut the smocking tape into two lengths equal to the width of one panel plus 2″ (5cm).

Press under 1″ (2.5cm) at the upper edge of one panel. Pin one length of smocking tape ¾″ (2cm) from the pressed edge. Press the ends of the tape under 1″ (2.5cm). Use a pin to pull out the smocking cords so that they are free from the folded ends. Referring to **Diagram 4,** stitch the tape in place along both long edges and at the ends. Stitch again in the middle of the tape and parallel to the long edges. Do not catch the smocking cords in the stitches. Repeat, applying the second length of smocking tape to the upper edge of the other panel.

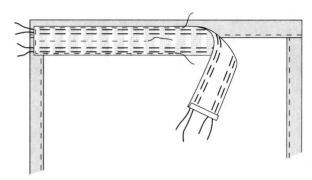

Diagram 4

Knot the smocking cords together at each side of one panel. Working on a flat surface, use one hand to pull up the cords. Use the other hand to guide the gathers along the tape, as shown in **Diagram 5.** Pull up the cords until the width of the panel is equal to half the circumference of the table. Loosely tie the cords together at the side of the panel to hold the gathers in place but do not cut the tails. Repeat for the other panel.

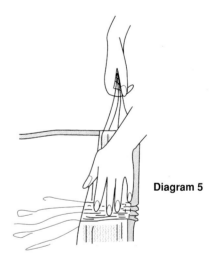

Diagram 5

🧵 SEW SIMPLE

Transform this dressing table skirt into a no-sew project. Hem the sides of the panel, following the directions on page 127 for no-sew hemming. To make the headers, use Dritz iron-on 2-cord shirring tape. Pull up the cords. Apply Dritz soft iron-on loop fastener tape over the gathers.

3 Installing the skirt

Apply the adhesive-backed hook tape in place around the outer edge of the table, ¾" (2cm) down from the upper edge.

Attach the skirt panels to the table, matching the smocking tape to the hook tape. Position the panels so that the side edges meet at the center front and center back of the table and the long smocking cord tails are at the center back.

⊕ DESIGN PLUS

With some minor adjustments, these instructions can be used to create a sink skirt. Before you begin, decide where the skirt panel will be installed.

- *If it will be installed on the outside of the sink, use the top outside edge of the sink, from wall to wall, as the circumference measurement.*

- *If it will be installed on the underside of a pedestal or wall-hung sink, use the measurement around the inside of the rim as the circumference measurement. Attach the hook tape to the inside of the rim. Measure from the top of the tape to the floor. Use this measurement plus 1¾" (4.5cm) for the cutting length.*

Baby will slip softly into slumberland surrounded by these custom-made crib bumpers, crib skirt, comforter, and tab-top cafés.

BEDTIME FOR BABY

CRIB BUMPERS

Size:

Two 10" × 5" (25.5cm × 130cm) side bumpers

Two 10" × 28" (25.5cm × 71cm) end bumpers

SUPPLIES

- *3⅞ yards (3.6m) of 45" (115cm) wide washable decorator fabric, such as chintz, sateen, broadcloth, or polished cotton**
- *1½ yards (1.4m) of 45" (115cm) wide polyester batting*
- *4¾ yards (4.4m) of ½" (1.3cm) diameter contrasting covered piping*
- *13½ yards (12.5m) of ½" (12mm) wide satin ribbon*
- *Water-soluble marking pen*

*See the "Cutting Directions" for additional information.

CUTTING DIRECTIONS

All measurements include ½" (1.3cm) seam allowances.

Before purchasing fabric, review the information on page 124 for working with printed fabrics.

From the decorator fabric, cut:

- *Eight 11" × 26½" (28cm × 67.5cm) side bumper panels*

- *Two 11" × 29" (28cm × 73.5cm) end bumper fronts*
- *Two 11" × 29" (28cm × 73.5cm) end bumper backs*

From the batting, cut:

- *Four 11" × 52" (28cm × 132cm) side batting sections*
- *Four 11" × 29" (28cm × 73.5cm) end batting sections*

From the satin ribbon, cut twenty 24" (61cm) long ties.

SEWING DIRECTIONS

1 Joining the side bumper panels

Referring to **Diagram 1,** with right sides together, stitch two side bumper panels together at the side edges to form one side bumper front. Press the seam open. Repeat, making one more side bumper front and two side bumper backs.

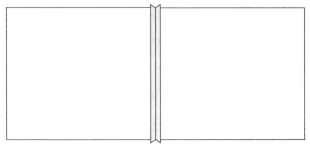

Diagram 1

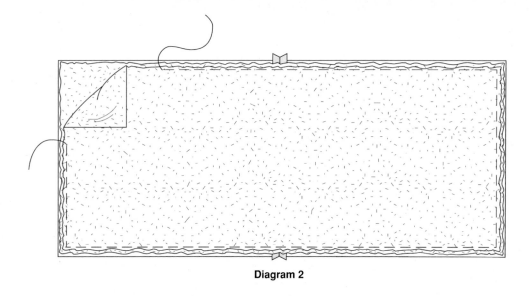

Diagram 2

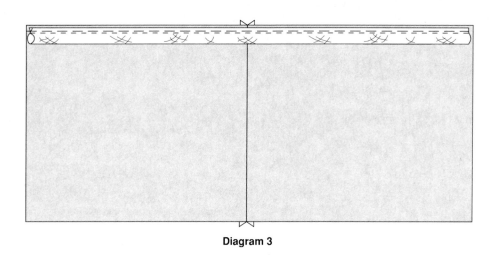

Diagram 3

2 Padding the bumpers

Pin one side batting section to the wrong side of the side bumper front. Pin another side batting section in place on top of the first one. Machine baste the layers together ⅜" (1cm) from the raw edges, as shown in **Diagram 2.** Repeat, padding the other side bumper front and the two end bumper fronts.

Referring to **Diagram 3,** on the right side of one side bumper front, machine baste the piping in place at the upper edge, following the directions on page 126 for applying piping. Repeat, basting piping in place at the upper edge of the other side bumper front and the two end bumper fronts.

✦ DESIGN PLUS

For custom-fitted bumpers, compare the width of your crib with our finished end bumper measurement and the length with our finished side bumper measurement. If necessary, adjust the cutting lengths of the bumper and batting sections.

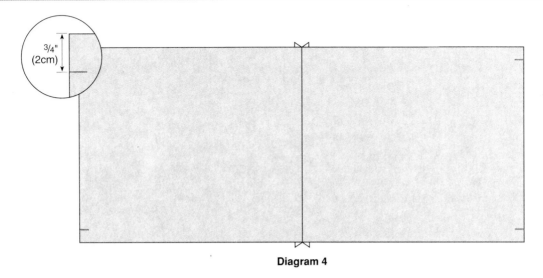

Diagram 4

3 Adding the ties

Using the marking pen, mark the tie placement on the right side of one side bumper back. Mark on the side edges ¾″ (2cm) from the long edges, as shown in **Diagram 4**. Repeat, marking the other side bumper back and the two end bumper backs.

Fold each ribbon tie in half so that the ends match. On one end bumper back, center one tie over each marked line, matching the folded ends of the ties to the raw edges of the bumper; machine baste the four ties in place, as shown in **Diagram 5**. Repeat for the

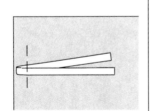

Diagram 5

other end bumper back and the two side bumper backs. On each side bumper back, center one tie over the seam line at the upper edge and another at the lower edge; machine baste in place.

4 Assembling the bumpers

With right sides together, pin together one side bumper front and one side bumper back. Stitch, being careful not to catch the ties in the stitching and leaving an opening along one long edge large enough for turning, as shown in **Diagram 6**. Trim the corners on the diagonal. Trim the batting close to the stitching. Turn the side bumper right side out. Slip stitch the opening closed, following the directions on page 125 for slip stitching. Repeat, assembling the other side bumper and the two end bumpers.

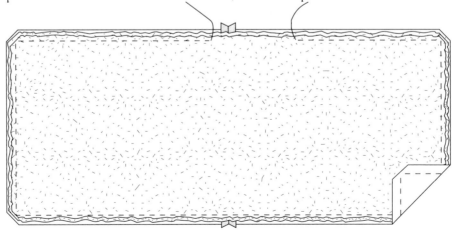

Diagram 6

5 Quilting the bumpers

Establish the quilting line on one end bumper by folding the bumper in half so that the side edges match. Use the marking pen to mark along the fold line. Unfold the bumper. Repeat, marking the quilting line on the other end bumper.

Establish the quilting lines on one side bumper by folding the bumper so that one side edge meets the center seam line. Use the marking pen to mark along the fold line. Repeat, folding the other side edge to meet the seam line and marking along the fold. Unfold the bumper. Repeat, marking quilting lines on the other side bumper.

Set the sewing machine stitch length for eight to ten stitches per inch (2.5cm). Referring to **Diagram 7,** machine stitch the side bumpers and the end bumpers along the marked lines, through all of the layers. Machine stitch each side bumper along the center seam line.

🧵 SEW SIMPLE

Fusible batting, such as Pellon Fusible Fleece, eliminates the need for machine basting. For best results, fuse one layer of batting to each bumper front and one layer to each bumper back.

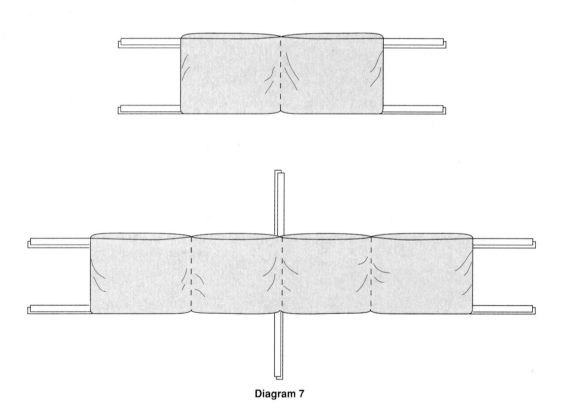

Diagram 7

GATHERED CRIB SKIRT

Size:

To fit a standard crib with a 28" × 51" (71cm × 130cm) mattress. The crib skirt measures 11" (28cm) long from the bottom of the mattress to the hem of the skirt.

SUPPLIES

- *2 yards (1.9m) of 45" to 60" (115cm to 153cm) wide decorator fabric, such as chintz, sateen, broadcloth, or polished cotton**
- *1½ yards (1.4m) of 45" (115cm) wide lining fabric, such as muslin, broadcloth, or polished cotton*
- *Water-soluble marking pen*

*See the "Cutting Directions" for additional information.

CUTTING DIRECTIONS

All measurements include ½" (1.3cm) seam allowances.

Before purchasing fabric, review the information on page 124 for working with printed fabrics.

From the decorator fabric, cut six 12" × 45" (30.5cm × 115cm) ruffle sections.

From the lining fabric, cut one 29" × 52" (73.5cm × 132cm) deck. Use the marking pen to divide and mark each edge of the deck into four equal parts.

✦ DESIGN PLUS

Add contrasting bands of ribbon to the lower edge of the ruffles.

SEWING DIRECTIONS

1 Joining the side ruffles

Referring to **Diagram 1,** with right sides together, stitch two ruffle sections together at the side edges to form one side ruffle. Repeat for the other side ruffle.

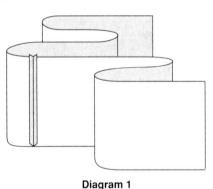

Diagram 1

2 Hemming the ruffles

Referring to **Diagram 2,** press under ½" (1.3cm) on one long edge of one side ruffle. Tuck the raw edge in to meet the crease. Press again. Stitch close to the second fold. Repeat, hemming one long edge and both side edges of the two side ruffles and the two end ruffles.

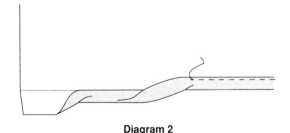

Diagram 2

3 Attaching the ruffles

Use the marking pen to mark each ruffle into four equal parts. Mark along the raw edges of the ruffles.

Machine baste along the raw edge of one ruffle, following the directions on page 125 for preparing a ruffle. Repeat, machine basting the other three ruffles.

Referring to **Diagram 3,** with right sides together, stitch one side ruffle to one long edge of the deck, placing the side edges of the ruffle ½" (1.3cm) in from the short edges of the deck, and then follow the directions on page 125 for gathering and attaching a ruffle. Repeat, stitching the other side ruffle and the two end ruffles to the deck.

Press the seams toward the wrong side of the deck. Stitch around the edge of the deck, as shown in **Diagram 4.**

SEW SIMPLE

Self-lined ruffles require a bit more fabric but eliminate time-consuming hems. Purchase 4 yards (3.7m) of decorator fabric. Cut six 23" × 45" (58.5cm × 115cm) ruffle sections. Join the side ruffles, following Step 1 of the "Sewing Directions." With wrong sides together, fold each ruffle in half lengthwise and stitch ½" (1.3cm) from the side edges. Turn the ruffles right side out and press. Attach the ruffles, following Step 3 of the "Sewing Directions."

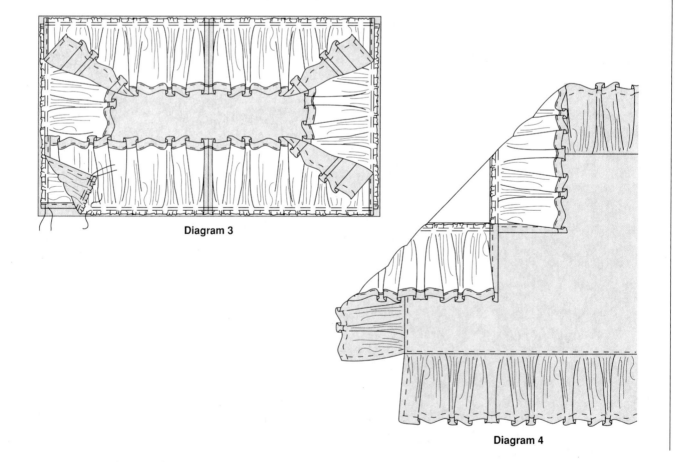

Diagram 3

Diagram 4

CRIB COMFORTER

Size:

33½″ × 43½″ (85cm × 111cm)

SUPPLIES

- *1 yard (1m) of 45″ (115cm) wide washable decorator fabric, such as chintz, sateen, broadcloth, or polished cotton*
- *1 yard (1m) of 45″ (115cm) wide contrasting washable decorator fabric*
- *2 yards (1.9m) of 45″ (115cm) wide polyester batting*
- *4⅝ yards (4.3m) of ½″ (1.3cm) diameter contrasting covered piping*
- *Water-soluble marking pen*
- *Yardstick*

CUTTING DIRECTIONS

All measurements include ½″ (1.3cm) seam allowances.

From the decorator fabric, cut one 35″ × 45″ (89cm × 115cm) front.

From the contrasting decorator fabric, cut one 35″ × 45″ (89cm × 115cm) back.

🧵 SEW SIMPLE

Preprinted fabric panels in nursery motifs are specially sized for small comforters. Choose one of these panels for the comforter front and a coordinating fabric for the back. Once the comforter is assembled, machine stitch around the edges of the printed design, through all of the layers.

From the batting, cut two 35″ × 45″ (89cm × 115cm) batting sections.

SEWING DIRECTIONS

1 Preparing the front

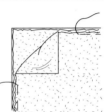

Pin one batting section to the wrong side of the front. Pin the second batting section in place on top of the first one. Machine baste the layers together ⅜″ (1cm) from the raw edges, as shown in **Diagram 1.**

Diagram 1

On the right side of the front, machine baste the piping in place around the edges, as shown in **Diagram 2** and following the directions on page 126 for applying piping.

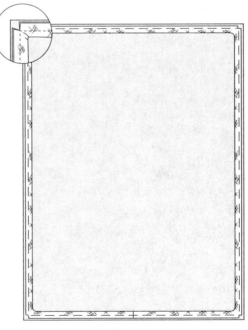

Diagram 2

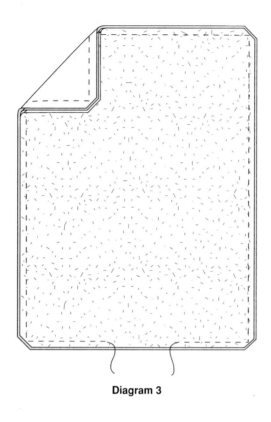

Diagram 3

Diagram 4

2 Assembling the comforter

With right sides together, stitch the front to the back, leaving a 10″ (25.5cm) opening at one edge large enough for turning, as shown in **Diagram 3.** Trim the corners on the diagonal. Trim the batting close to the stitching.

Turn the comforter right side out. Slip stitch the opening closed, following the directions on page 125 for slip stitching.

3 Quilting the comforter

Working on a large, flat surface, use long hand stitches to baste the comforter layers together. Work from the center out to each corner and then from the center out to each edge, as shown in **Diagram 4.**

Use the yardstick and the marking pen to draw vertical quilting lines on the front of the quilt. Place

the lines about 2″ (5cm) apart and parallel to the side edges.

Set the sewing machine stitch length for eight to ten stitches per inch (2.5cm). Machine stitch along the quilting lines, through all of the layers.

⊕ DESIGN PLUS

The appliqués that adorn the shower curtain, bath mat, and towels in the photograph on page 82 would look equally at home in the nursery. Use the bear and the balloon appliqués (see Diagrams 4 and 5 on page 85) on the comforter. Apply the shapes to the comforter front, following the directions on pages 84 to 86, before applying the batting. Adjust the position of the shapes so that they fit inside the seam lines. Decorate the crib bumpers and the tab-top cafés with the small balloon appliqués (see Diagram 1 on page 88).

TAB-TOP CAFÉS

Window Size:

24" to 40" (61cm to 102cm) wide × 50" (127cm) long

SUPPLIES

- 2⅞ yards (2.7m) of 45" (115cm) wide decorator fabric, such as chintz, sateen, broadcloth, or polished cotton
- 2½ yards (2.3m) each of two colors of ⅜" (9mm) wide satin ribbon
- 1 café curtain rod
- 1 spring tension rod
- Water-soluble marking pen

CUTTING DIRECTIONS

All measurements include ½" (1.3cm) seam allowances.

From the decorator fabric, cut the following pieces, as shown in **Diagram 1:**

- *Two 30" × 33" (76cm × 84cm) curtains*
- *One 19" × 45" (48.5cm × 115cm) valance*

From the remaining decorator fabric, cut nineteen 4" × 7" (10cm × 18cm) tabs.

SEWING DIRECTIONS

1 Making the tabs

With right sides together, fold each tab in half lengthwise. Stitch the long edges together, as shown in **Diagram 2.**

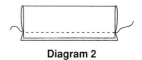

Diagram 2

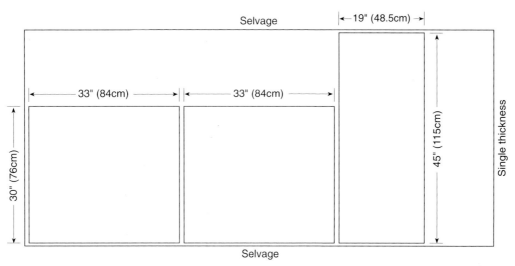

Diagram 1

Turn each tab right side out. Press. Fold each tab in half crosswise, as shown in **Diagram 3,** and machine baste the raw edges together.

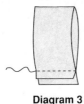

Diagram 3

2 Hemming the edges

Referring to **Diagram 4,** press under 3″ (7.5cm) on the lower edge of the valance. Tuck the raw edge in to meet the crease. Press again. Stitch close to the second fold.

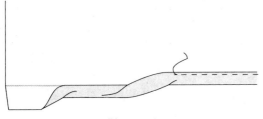

Diagram 4

Press under 6″ (15cm) on the lower edge of one curtain. Tuck the raw edge in to meet the crease. Press again. Stitch close to the second fold. Repeat, hemming the lower edge of the other curtain.

Press under 1″ (2.5cm) on one side edge of the valance. Tuck the raw edge in to meet the crease. Press again. Stitch close to the second fold. Repeat, hemming the other side edge of the valance and the side edges of both curtains.

3 Creating the facings

Referring to **Diagram 5,** measure and then use the marking pen to mark 2½″ (6.3cm) from the upper edge across the valance. Cut along the marked line, creating the valance facing.

Repeat, creating a curtain facing for each curtain.

4 Applying the tabs

On the right side of the valance, pin and then machine baste nine tabs across the upper edge of the valance, evenly spacing them, as shown in **Diagram 6.** The raw edges of the tabs should be even with the raw edge of the valance.

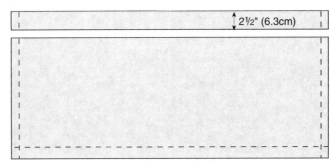

2½″ (6.3cm)

Diagram 5

Diagram 6

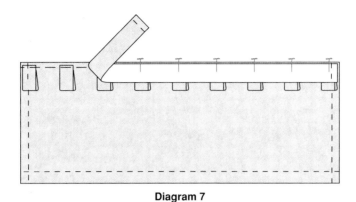

Diagram 7

Repeat for both curtains, evenly spacing five tabs across the upper edge of each curtain.

5 Attaching the facing

With right sides together and the tabs in between, pin the valance facing to the valance with raw edges and side edges even, as shown in **Diagram 7.** Stitch across the upper edge of the valance. Press the seam open and then press the facing to the wrong side of the valance.

Referring to **Diagram 8,** tuck the lower edge of the facing in to meet the raw edges of the seam allowances. Press. Stitch close to the fold, through the valance and the facing.

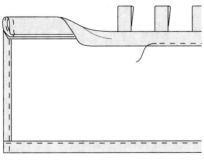

Diagram 8

Repeat for both curtains, stitching the curtain facings to the upper edges of the curtains.

6 Applying the bows

Cut the ribbon into nineteen 9″ (23cm) lengths. Tie each length into a bow, following the directions on page 128 for tying a bow. Sew a bow in place at the front lower edge of each tab, alternating the colors, as shown in the photograph on page 52.

INSTALLATION

Install the café rod on the wall above the window. Install the spring tension rod at the middle of the window. Hang the valance and the curtains on the rods, as shown in the photograph on page 52.

🧵 SEW SIMPLE

Use small, nonrusting safety pins to attach the bows. This cuts down on sewing time and makes it easy to remove the bows at laundry time.

A *stenciled floral design converts standard sheets and pillowcases into designer-quality bed linens, matching headboard, and decorator pillow.*

A BED OF ROSES

PADDED HEADBOARD

Size:

To fit a standard twin-size, double, queen-size, or king-size bed

SUPPLIES

- *1 white flat sheet**
- *One 4 × 8 sheet of ½" (1.3cm) thick plywood**
- *1 sheet of 1" (2.5cm) thick foam rubber**
- *Polyester batting**
- *Brown paper or craft paper**
- *Tissue paper (optional)*
- *Two ¾" × 4" × 36" (2cm × 10cm × 91.5cm) wood boards*
- *Sandpaper*
- *Wood sealer*
- *White paint*
- *Paintbrush*
- *Rubber cement*
- *Water-soluble marking pen*
- *Staple gun*
- *Drill with ⅜" (1cm) bit*

- *Four ⅜" (1cm) screws*
- *Two ⅜" (1cm) nuts and bolts*
- *Saber saw*
- *Serrated knife*

STENCILING

- *Oiled stencil paper or stencil acetate*
- *Graphite paper for transferring the designs*
- *Craft knife*
- *Three ½" (1.3cm) flat stencil brushes*
- *3 colors of stencil paint (here, we used dark green, dark red, and medium blue)*
- *Soap and water or turpentine to clean brushes, as directed by the paint manufacturer*
- *Fixative spray, such as Krylon*

*See the "Cutting Directions" for additional information.

CUTTING DIRECTIONS

All measurements include ½" (1.3cm) seam allowances.

The size of the bed determines the size of the flat sheet as well as the dimensions for the paper pattern, plywood, foam rubber, and batting. Consult the chart on page 66 to determine the dimensions for each item. Note: It may be necessary to piece the foam.

	BED SIZE (W × L)	SHEET SIZE	PAPER	PLYWOOD AND FOAM RUBBER	BATTING
Twin	39″ × 75″ (99cm × 191cm)	Twin	24½″ × 40″ (62cm × 102cm)	30″ × 39″ (76cm × 99cm)	36″ × 45″ (91.5cm × 115cm)
Double	54″ × 75″ (138cm × 191cm)	Twin	32″ × 40″ (81.5cm × 102cm)	30″ × 54″ (76cm × 138cm)	36″ × 60″ (91.5cm × 153cm)
Queen	60″ × 80″ (153cm × 204cm)	Full	35″ × 40″ (89cm × 102cm)	30″ × 60″ (76cm × 153cm)	36″ × 66″ (91.5cm × 168cm)
King	78″ × 80″ (199cm × 204cm)	Queen	40″ × 44″ (102cm × 112cm)	30″ × 78″ (76cm × 199cm)	36″ × 84″ (91.5cm × 214cm)

Referring to **Diagram 1** and using the size craft paper that corresponds to your bed size, make a pattern for the headboard sections. Round off the upper left corner. Label the right side with the "place on fold" line. Draw three parallel lines that are 2″, 4″, and 5″ (5cm, 10cm, and 12.5cm) from the upper, lower, and left side edges, respectively.

- *Label the outer edge for the front cover pattern.*
- *Label the 2″ (5cm) line for the batting pattern.*
- *Label the 4″ (10cm) line for the back cover pattern.*
- *Label the 5″ (12.5cm) line for the base pattern.*

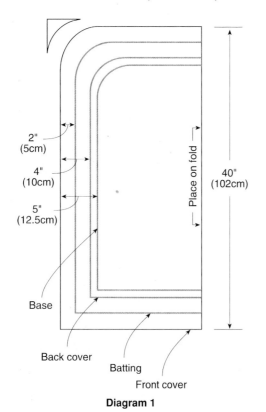

Diagram 1

If desired, use tissue paper to trace a separate pattern for the back cover.

Fold the flat sheet in half lengthwise. Pin the pattern in place, matching the pattern fold line to the fabric fold, as shown in **Diagram 2.** Cut one front cover.

Fold the polyester batting in half. Pin the pattern in place, matching the pattern fold line to the batting fold. Cut one batting section. Repeat, cutting one back cover from the remaining flat sheet.

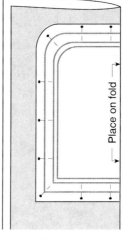

Diagram 2

Referring to **Diagram 3,** trace the cutting line for the base onto the plywood. Flip the pattern over and trace the other half. Cut out the base, using the saw.

Diagram 3

ASSEMBLY DIRECTIONS

1 Drilling mounting holes in the base

Measure the distance between the headboard mounting slots on the bed frame (A), as shown in **Diagram 4.**

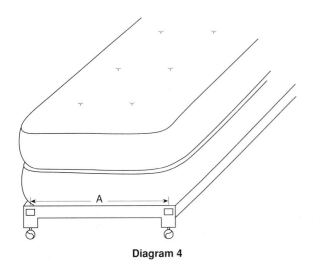

Diagram 4

Referring to **Diagram 5,** mark the lengthwise center of the base. Make one set of marks on each side of the base 3″ (7.5cm) and 13″ (33cm) above the lower edge. The distance between the center line and each set of side marks should equal one-half of A plus 1″ (2.5cm). Drill a ⅜″ (1cm) leg mounting hole at each side mark.

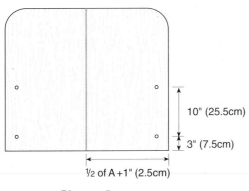

10″ (25.5cm)

3″ (7.5cm)

½ of A +1″ (2.5cm)

Diagram 5

2 Drilling mounting holes in the leg boards

Referring to **Diagram 6,** mark the lengthwise center of one board. Mark along the center line 2″ (5cm) and 12″ (30.5cm) below the upper edge of the board for the leg mounting holes. Mark a ⅜″ (1cm) wide × 6″ (15cm) long headboard mounting slot, placing the slot 3″ (7.5cm) up from the lower edge and 1″ (2.5cm) in from the inside edge. Mark the other leg board as a mirror image of the first. Drill a ⅜″ (1cm) hole at each leg mounting mark. Drill a pilot hole to start the slots; then use the saw to cut them out.

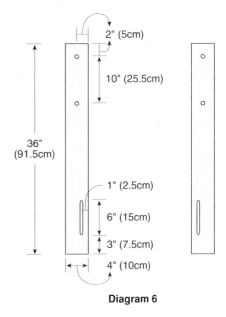

2″ (5cm)

10″ (25.5cm)

36″ (91.5cm)

1″ (2.5cm)

6″ (15cm)

3″ (7.5cm)

4″ (10cm)

Diagram 6

3 Painting the base and the leg boards

Sand the base and the leg boards. Apply the wood sealer, following the manufacturer's directions. Paint the boards white.

4 Attaching the foam rubber

Apply rubber cement to the front of the base. Smooth the foam in place over the cement. If it is necessary to piece the foam, butt the edges together (see **Diagram 7**). Using the serrated knife, trim the foam evenly with the edge of the plywood.

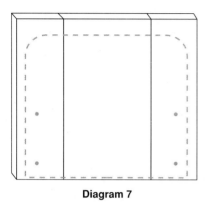

Diagram 7

5 Attaching the batting

Center the base, foam side down, on the batting. Beginning at the center top and bottom, wrap and staple the batting to the back of the base. Wrap and staple the center of each side edge in the same way, as shown in **Diagram 8.** Working from the center out toward each corner, continue wrapping and stapling the batting to the back of the base. Stop stapling 3″ (7.5cm) from the lower corners and 8″ (20.5cm) from the upper corners.

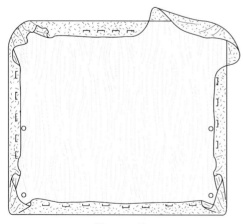

Diagram 8

Referring to **Diagram 9,** wrap and staple the batting at each corner as follows: Staple the batting at the center of the corner. Fold in the fullness on each side of the center and staple. Continue, alternating from side to side, until all of the batting is stapled in place. If necessary, cut out wedges of excess batting to reduce bulk.

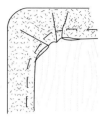

Diagram 9

6 Attaching the front cover

Fold the front cover in half lengthwise and crosswise. Using the marking pen, mark the folds at the fabric edges to divide the cover into quarters. Unfold the cover.

Machine baste around the front cover, stitching 1″ (2.5cm) and ½″ (1.3cm) from the edge. Break the stitching at the marks, as shown in **Diagram 10.**

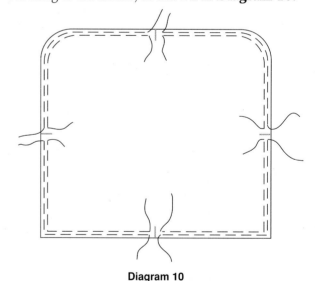

Diagram 10

Place the front cover wrong side up on a flat surface. Center the base, padded side down, on the front cover. Draw up the basting stitches, shaping the cover to fit around each corner, as shown in **Diagram 11.**

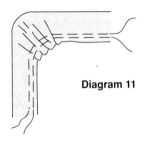

Diagram 11

Wrap and staple the cover to the back of the base, following the same sequence as for wrapping and stapling the batting.

7 Attaching the back cover

Center the back cover right side up on the back of the base. Fold the raw edges under, covering the staples and the raw edges of the front cover and batting. Staple the back cover to the headboard, as shown in **Diagram 12.**

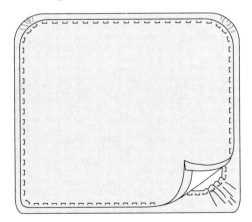

Diagram 12

🧵 SEW SIMPLE

Use push pins or tacks to temporarily baste tack the front cover in place on the back of the base. Turn over the headboard and check to be sure the fabric is smooth and taut before permanently stapling the cover in place.

STENCILING DIRECTIONS

1 Preparing the stencils

Photocopy **Diagrams 13** and **14** on page 70 enlarging them as indicated.

Review the information on page 127 in "Stenciling." Using the enlarged diagrams, prepare the stencils for the corner and center designs as directed.

2 Applying the designs

At one upper corner of the front cover, position the corner stencil about 3″ (7.5cm) from the headboard edges, as shown in the photograph on page 64. Stencil the leaves first, using the dark green paint. Stencil all of the roses, plus some of the small buds and flowers, using the dark red paint. Stencil the ribbons and the remaining flowers and buds, using the medium blue paint. Reverse the stencil and repeat for the other upper corner.

Center the center stencil on the front cover 3″ (7.5cm) below the upper edge of the headboard. Stencil the design, following the same sequence as for the corners.

Following the manufacturer's directions, apply the fixative spray to the finished designs.

INSTALLATION

Using the screws, attach the leg boards to the back of the headboard at the mounting holes. Using the nuts and bolts, attach the leg boards to the back of the bed frame at the slots, adjusting the headboard to the desired height.

Note: Diagrams 13 and 14 are one-half the actual size.
Photocopy the diagrams, enlarging them 200%.

Diagram 13

Diagram 14

BED LINENS

Size:

To fit a standard twin-size, double, queen-size, or king-size bed

SUPPLIES

- *1 white flat sheet**
- *2 white standard- or king-size pillowcases*
- *1¾" (4.5cm) wide white lace edging**
- *⅞" (23mm) wide blue satin ribbon**
- *2 small ribbon roses*

STENCILING

- *Oiled stencil paper or stencil acetate*
- *Graphite paper for transferring the design*
- *Craft knife*
- *Three ½" (1.3cm) flat stencil brushes*
- *3 colors of stencil paint (here, we used dark green, dark red, and medium blue)*
- *Soap and water or turpentine to clean brushes, as directed by the paint manufacturer*
- *Fixative spray, such as Krylon*

*See the "Cutting Directions" for additional information.

CUTTING DIRECTIONS

The size of the flat sheet determines how much 1¾" (4.5cm) wide lace edging and ⅞" (23mm) wide ribbon are required.

- *For one twin-size flat sheet and two pillowcases, purchase 8½ yards (7.9m) of lace edging and 4⅞ yards (4.5m) of ribbon.*

- *For one full-size flat sheet and two pillowcases, purchase 9 yards (8.3m) of lace edging and 5¼ yards (4.9m) of ribbon.*

- *For one queen-size flat sheet and two pillowcases, purchase 9¾ yards (9m) of lace edging and 5½ yards (5.1m) of ribbon.*

- *For one king-size flat sheet and two pillowcases, purchase 10⅝ yards (9.8m) of lace edging and 6 yards (5.5m) of ribbon.*

STENCILING DIRECTIONS

1 Preparing the stencils

Photocopy **Diagrams 13** and **14** on page 70, enlarging them as indicated.

Review the information on page 127 in "Stenciling." Using the enlarged diagrams, prepare the stencils for the corner and center designs as directed.

2 Stenciling the sheet

Fold the sheet in half lengthwise and pin mark the center at the upper edge of the sheet. Unfold the sheet.

Referring to **Diagram 1** on page 72, position the center stencil so that it is centered and 5" (12.5cm) from the hemmed edge on the right side of the sheet. Stencil the leaves first, using the dark green paint. Stencil all of the roses, plus some of the small buds and flowers, using the dark red paint. Stencil the ribbons and the remaining flowers and buds, using the medium blue paint.

Following the manufacturer's directions, apply the fixative spray to the finished design.

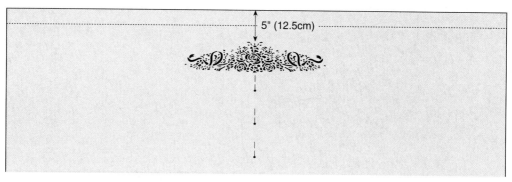

5" (12.5cm)

Diagram 1

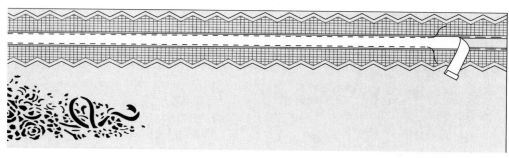

Diagram 2

3 Stenciling the pillowcases

Position the corner stencil 2″ (5cm) in from the side and 2″ (5cm) from one long edge of one pillowcase, as shown in the photograph on page 64. Apply the stencil paint in the same sequence as for the sheet. Reverse the stencil and repeat for the diagonally opposite corner, positioning the stencil 5″ (12.5cm) from the hemmed edge and 2″ (5cm) from the long edge of the pillowcase. Repeat, stenciling the other pillowcase.

Following the manufacturer's directions, apply the fixative spray to the finished designs.

✦ DESIGN PLUS

For a bit of old-world charm, use off-white sheets. Add matching lace trim or new white lace "antiqued" by dipping it in a strong tea solution. For better color retention, use 100 percent cotton or 90 percent cotton/10 percent nylon lace trims.

SEWING DIRECTIONS

1 Trimming the sheet

Cut two pieces of lace and one piece of ribbon, each equal to the width of the sheet plus 1″ (2.5cm).

Referring to **Diagram 2,** pin the lace to the upper edge of the sheet, above the stenciled design, positioning the lace so that the straight edges face each other and are ¾″ (2cm) apart. Turn the ends under ½″ (1.3cm). Machine baste the lace in place along the straight edges.

Center the ribbon over the space between the lace and turn the ends under ½″ (1.3cm). Stitch along both edges of the ribbon, securing the ribbon and the lace.

2 Trimming the pillowcases

Cut four pieces of lace and two pieces of ribbon, each 41″ (104cm) long.

Referring to **Diagram 3,** pin two pieces of lace around the hemmed edge of one pillowcase, positioning the lace so that the straight edges face

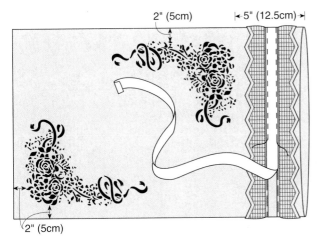

2" (5cm) |←5" (12.5cm)→|

2" (5cm)

Diagram 3

each other and are ¾" (2cm) apart. Overlap the ends of the lace on the back of the pillowcase. Machine baste the lace in place along the straight edges. Center one piece of ribbon over the space between the lace, overlapping the ends on the back of the pillowcase and turning the raw edge under. Stitch along both edges of the ribbon, securing the ribbon and the lace. Repeat for the other pillowcase.

Cut the remaining ribbon in half. Tie each piece into a bow, following the directions on page 128 for tying a bow. Sew one bow in place at the center front of each pillowcase, over the ribbon trim. Sew a ribbon rose in place at the center of each bow.

DECORATOR PILLOW

Size:

12" (30.5cm) square

SUPPLIES

- *1 white standard-size pillowcase*
- *2¾ yards (2.6m) of 1¾" (4.5cm) wide white lace edging*
- *One 12" (30.5cm) square pillow form*
- *Seam ripper or small scissors*

STENCILING

- *Oiled stencil paper or stencil acetate*
- *Graphite paper for transferring the design*
- *Craft knife*
- *Three ½" (1.3cm) flat stencil brushes*
- *3 colors of stencil paint (here, we used dark green, dark red, and medium blue)*
- *Soap and water or turpentine to clean brushes, as directed by the paint manufacturer*
- *Fixative spray, such as Krylon*

CUTTING DIRECTIONS

All measurements include ½" (1.3cm) seam allowances.

Using a seam ripper or small scissors, rip out the pillowcase seam. Press the pillowcase flat. From the pillowcase, cut two 13" (33cm) squares for the cover front and cover back.

🧵 SEW SIMPLE

If desired, purchase 1⅝ yards (1.5m) of gathered lace trim instead of the flat lace edging. Join the ends and baste the trim in place, following the technique illustrated in Diagram 4 on page 75.

STENCILING DIRECTIONS

1 Preparing the stencil

Photocopy **Diagram 1,** enlarging it as indicated.

Note: Diagram is one-half the actual size.
Photocopy the diagram, enlarging it 200%.

Diagram 1

Review the information on page 127 in "Stenciling." Using the enlarged diagram, prepare the bouquet stencil as directed.

⊕ DESIGN PLUS

Use the coordinating stencil patterns in **Diagrams 13** *and* **14** *on page 70 to adorn additional decorator pillows in graduated sizes. Group them attractively at the head of the bed.*

---

2 Applying the design

Pin mark the center of one fabric square. On the right side of the fabric, position the stencil to the right of the center, as shown in **Diagram 2.** Stencil the leaves first, using the dark green paint. Stencil the flowers and some of the buds, using the dark red paint. Stencil the ribbons and the remaining buds, using the medium blue paint.

Diagram 2

Reverse the stencil. Position it to the left of the center, slightly overlapping it onto the ribbon loops of the first motif, as shown in the photograph on page 64. Stencil the design, following the same sequence as for the first motif.

Following the manufacturer's directions, apply the fixative spray to the finished design.

SEWING DIRECTIONS

1 Preparing the ruffle

With right sides together, stitch the ends of the lace together to form a continuous piece, as shown in **Diagram 3.** Press the seam open.

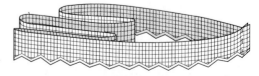

Diagram 3

Machine baste along the straight edge of the lace, following the directions on page 125 for preparing a ruffle.

Divide and mark the ruffle into eight equal parts.

2 Applying the ruffle

Mark the center of each edge of the cover front. Referring to **Diagram 4,** with right sides together, baste the ruffle to the cover front. Follow the directions on page 125 for gathering and attaching a ruffle, matching the ruffle marks to the cover front corners and center marks.

Diagram 4

3 Finishing the cover

With right sides together, pin the cover front and back together. Stitch, leaving an opening along one side large enough for turning and inserting the pillow form. Trim the corners, as shown in **Diagram 5.**

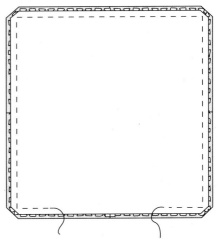

Diagram 5

Turn the cover right side out. Press. Insert the pillow form through the opening. Slip stitch the opening closed, following the directions on page 125 for slip stitching.

A custom-fitted, reversible canopy with ruffled edges is the crowning glory for a four-poster bed.

FLOWER BOWER

Size:

To fit a standard twin-size, double, queen-size, or king-size bed with a flat canopy frame

SUPPLIES

- *45" or 54" (115cm or 138cm) wide decorator fabric, such as chintz, sateen, or polished cotton**
- *45" or 54" (115cm or 138cm) wide contrasting decorator fabric**
- *45" or 54" (115cm or 138cm) wide lining fabric, such as chintz, sateen, or polished cotton**
- *Water-soluble marking pen*

*See the "Cutting Directions" for additional information.

CUTTING DIRECTIONS

All measurements include ½" (1.3cm) seam allowances.

Consult the chart to determine how much decorator fabric (for the top), contrasting decorator fabric (for the ruffle), and lining fabric (for the top lining and the ruffle lining) to purchase for your size bed. Before purchasing fabric, review the information on page 124 for working with printed fabrics.

For a twin-size bed:

- *From the decorator fabric, cut one 37" × 76" (94cm × 193cm) top. Repeat, cutting the top lining from the lining fabric.*
- *From the contrasting decorator fabric, cut ten 14" (35.5cm) long ruffle sections. Use the full width of the fabric as the width of each ruffle section. Repeat, cutting the ruffle lining sections from the lining fabric.*

For a double bed:

- *From the decorator fabric, if using 45" (115cm) wide fabric, cut one 45" × 76" (115cm × 193cm) top center panel and two 6" × 76" (15cm × 193cm) top side panels. If using 54" (138cm) wide decorator fabric, cut one 54" × 76" (138cm × 193cm) top center panel. Repeat, cutting the top lining panels from the lining fabric.*
- *From the contrasting decorator fabric, cut eleven 14" (35.5cm) long ruffle sections. Use the full width of the fabric as the width of each ruffle section. Repeat, cutting the ruffle lining.*

BED SIZE		YARDAGE		
	(W × L)	TOP	RUFFLE	LINING
Twin	39" × 75" (99cm × 191cm)	2⅛ yards (2m)	4 yards* (3.7m)	6⅛ yards* (5.7m)
Double	54" × 75" (138cm × 191cm)	4¼ yards (3.9cm)	4⅜ yards* (4.1m)	8⅝ yards* (8m)
Queen	60" × 80" (153cm × 204cm)	4½ yards (4.2m)	4¾ yards* (4.4m)	9¼ yards* (8.6m)
King	78" × 80" (199cm × 204cm)	4½ yards (4.2m)	5½ yards* (5.1m)	10 yards* (9.3m)

*If the contrasting decorator fabric and the lining fabric are not the same width, trim the wider fabric to match the narrower one before cutting out the ruffle and the ruffle lining sections.

For a queen-size bed:

- *From the decorator fabric, cut one 45" × 81" (115cm × 206cm) top center panel and two 9" × 81" (23cm × 206cm) top side panels. Repeat, cutting the top lining panels from the lining fabric.*

- *From the contrasting decorator fabric, cut twelve 14" (35.5cm) long ruffle sections. Use the full width of the fabric as the width of each ruffle section. Repeat, cutting the ruffle lining sections from the lining fabric.*

For a king-size bed:

- *From the decorator fabric, cut one 45" × 81" (115cm × 206cm) top center panel and two 17" × 81" (43cm × 206cm) top side panels. Repeat, cutting the top lining panels from the lining fabric.*

- *From the contrasting decorator fabric, cut fourteen 14" (35.5cm) long ruffle sections. Use the full width of the fabric as the width of each ruffle section. Repeat, cutting the ruffle lining sections from the lining fabric.*

SEWING DIRECTIONS

1 Assembling the top and the lining

For a double, queen-, or king-size bed, with right sides together, stitch one top side panel to each side edge of the top center panel, as shown in **Diagram 1.** Press the seams open. Repeat for the lining panels.

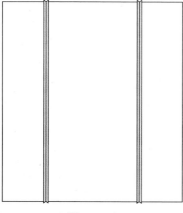

Diagram 1

For all size beds, divide and mark the edge of the top into eight equal parts.

2 Marking the finial openings

Unscrew the finial from the top of each canopy post. Referring to **Diagram 2,** measure the distance in from the outer edge of each post to the finial screw. To accommodate for the seam allowances on the canopy top, add ½" (1.3cm) to each measurement. Working on the right side of the canopy top, use the marking pen to mark for a finial opening at each corner, as shown in **Diagram 3.**

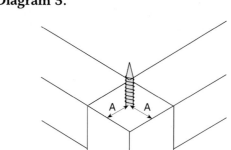

Diagram 2

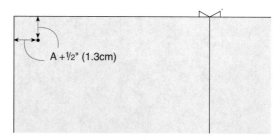

Diagram 3

🧵 SEW SIMPLE

To customize this canopy to fit an arched frame, measure the length of the frame along the top of the arch. Compare this measurement plus 1" (2.5cm) for seam allowances with the top center panel cutting length listed in the "Cutting Directions" for your size bed. Purchase additional decorator fabric and lining fabric to accommodate the extra length.

3 Assembling the ruffle

Referring to **Diagram 4,** with right sides together, stitch the ruffle sections together at the ends to form one continuous ruffle. Press the seams open. Repeat for the ruffle lining sections.

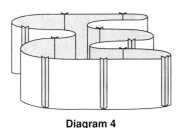

Diagram 4

With right sides together, stitch the ruffle to the ruffle lining along one long edge, as shown in **Diagram 5.** Turn the ruffle right side out and press.

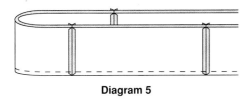

Diagram 5

Machine baste along the raw edges through both layers, following the directions on page 125 for preparing a ruffle.

4 Attaching the ruffle

Divide and mark the ruffle into eight equal parts.

Referring to **Diagram 6,** with right sides together, machine baste the ruffle to the top, following the directions on page 125 for gathering and attaching a ruffle.

✤ DESIGN PLUS

This reversible canopy provides several mix 'n' match possibilities. Consider using the same fabric for the top and the ruffle, and a coordinating one for the lining. Or use four coordinating fabrics—one each for the top, top lining, ruffle, and ruffle lining.

Purchase extra fabric or use the leftovers from a double, queen-size, or king-size canopy to make coordinating decorator pillows. For inspiration, check out the pillow projects on pages 13, 27, and 41.

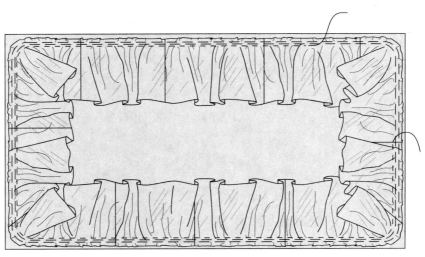

Diagram 6

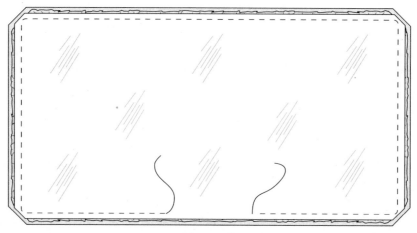

Diagram 7

5 Attaching the lining

With right sides together and raw edges even, stitch the top lining to the top, leaving an 8″ (20.5cm) opening at one edge, as shown in **Diagram 7.** Trim the corners on the diagonal. Turn the canopy right side out and remove the safety pins. Slip stitch the opening closed, following the directions on page 125 for slip stitching.

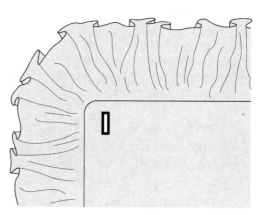

Diagram 8

6 Making the finial openings

Make one ¾″ (2cm) long machine buttonhole at each finial marking, centering the buttonhole over the marking, as shown in **Diagram 8.**

7 Installing the canopy

Drape the canopy over the frame, inserting a finial screw through each buttonhole opening. Screw the finials back onto the posts.

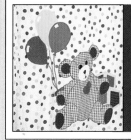 # BATH TIME

A *balloon-bearing teddy is the focal point of a cheerful ensemble that includes shower curtain, towels, and bath mat.*

BEARING UP

SHOWER CURTAIN

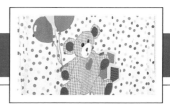

Size:

72" (183cm) square

SUPPLIES

- 4½ yards (4.2m) of 45" to 60" (115cm to 153cm) wide light- to medium-weight fabric, such as broadcloth, calico, or gingham
- 12 large grommets
- Plastic shower curtain liner and 12 rod hooks
- Water-soluble marking pen

APPLIQUÉ (optional)

- ¾ yard (0.7m) of 45" (115cm) wide red gingham
- ⅜ yard (0.4m) each of 45" (115cm) wide blue, red, yellow, and green broadcloth
- 7" (18cm) square of white broadcloth
- 4" (10cm) square of black broadcloth
- ¾ yard (0.7m) of red baby rickrack
- ¼ yard (0.3m) of ⅞" (23mm) wide red satin ribbon
- 2¼ yards (2.1m) each of yellow and green maxi-rickrack
- 2 yards (1.9m) of 45" (115cm) wide nonwoven pattern-duplicating material
- 2 yards (1.9m) of 18" (45.5cm) wide paper-backed fusible web
- 2 yards (1.9m) of 22" (56cm) wide tear-away stabilizer
- 1 spool each of blue, green, red, yellow, black, and white machine embroidery thread
- Glue stick
- Pencil

CUTTING DIRECTIONS

All measurements include ½" (1.3cm) seam allowances.

From the light- to medium-weight fabric, cut one 80" (204cm) long center panel from the full width of the fabric. Split the remaining fabric in half lengthwise and cut two 80" (204cm) long side panels.

SEWING DIRECTIONS

1 Joining the panels

With right sides together, stitch one side panel to each side edge of the center panel, as shown in **Diagram 1.** Press the seams open. Cut an equal amount from each side edge so that the joined panels measure 76" (193cm) wide.

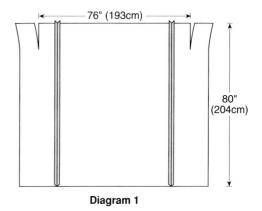

Diagram 1

2 Hemming the curtain

Referring to **Diagram 2,** press
under 2″ (5cm) on one side
edge. Tuck the raw edge in to
meet the crease. Press again.
Stitch close to the second fold.
Repeat for the other side edge.

Press under 4″ (10cm) on the
lower edge. Tuck the raw edge
in to meet the crease. Press
again. Stitch close to the second
fold. Repeat for the upper edge.

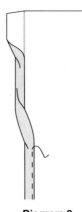

Diagram 2

3 Attaching the grommets

Working on the right side of the curtain, use the
marking pen to mark the grommet placement
across the top, as shown in **Diagram 3**. Place one
mark ¾″ (2cm) in from each side edge.

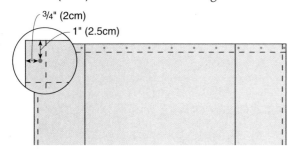

Diagram 3

Place ten more marks at evenly spaced intervals
(approximately 6½″ [16.5cm] apart) between the
first two marks. Place each mark 1″ (2.5cm) from
the upper edge of the curtain.

Attach one grommet at each mark, following the
grommet manufacturer's directions.

APPLIQUÉ DIRECTIONS

1 Creating the appliqué shapes

Using the pattern-duplicating material, create the
appliqué patterns shown in **Diagrams 4** and **5** on
page 85, enlarging the patterns as indicated. Using
the pencil, trace each appliqué pattern onto the

paper side of the fusible web. Cut out each
appliqué shape, leaving a margin of fusible web
all around the traced outline. Do not remove the
paper backings.

Referring to the photograph on page 82, apply
each appliqué shape to the wrong side of the
corresponding fabric, following the fusible web
manufacturer's directions. Cut out each appliqué
shape on the traced outline.

2 Fusing the appliqué shapes

Peel off the paper backings and fuse the appliqué
shapes to the center of the curtain, following
the fusible web manufacturer's directions and the
numerical order shown in **Diagram 6.**

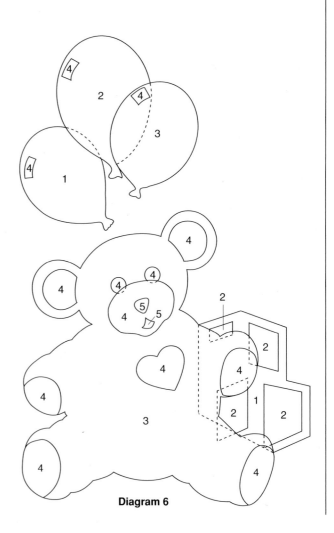

Diagram 6

Position the bottom of the bear approximately 16″ (40.5cm) above the lower edge of the curtain. Position the balloons approximately 12″ to 18″ (30.5cm to 45.5cm) above one paw. Note: The dashed lines indicate where the appliqués overlap.

Use the marking pen to draw the remaining details, as indicated by the dotted lines in **Diagram 5.**

⊕ DESIGN PLUS

When light-color appliqué shapes are fused to a print background fabric, the background motif may create shadows on the finished appliqué. To find out if this will be a problem, test fuse, applying scraps of the gingham, white, and yellow appliqué fabrics to scraps of the shower curtain fabric. If the print motif is visible, use a light- to medium-weight fusible interfacing to solve the problem. Apply it to the wrong side of the appliqué fabrics before applying the paper-backed fusible web.

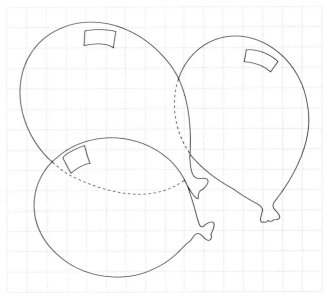

One square = 1″ (2.5cm)   **Diagram 4**

Appliqué Pattern Key

—————— Tracing line

- - - - - - Tracing line
(will be hidden
behind fabric)

·············· Stitching line
(for detail
stitching only)

Note: Because the patterns will be traced onto the back of the paper-backed fusible web, they are mirror images of the finished appliqué.

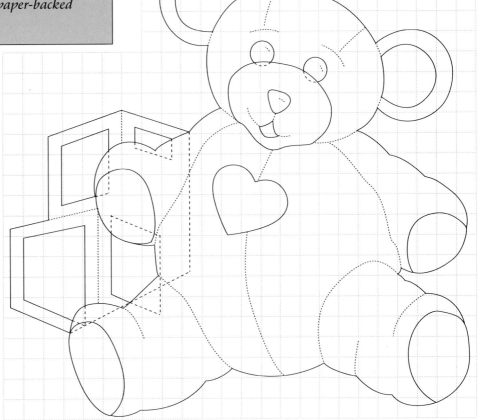

One square = 1″ (2.5cm)   **Diagram 5**

3 Stitching the appliqué shapes

Cut a piece of tear-away stabilizer that is slightly larger than the bear and the blocks. Center the stabilizer over the bear and the blocks on the wrong side of the curtain. Hand baste it in place. Repeat, applying tear-away stabilizer to the back of the balloon appliqués. Note: If necessary, use two pieces of stabilizer under the bear, slightly overlapping the cut edges.

Using a short, wide machine zigzag stitch and referring to the directions on page 126 for machine appliqué, stitch the appliqué shapes to the curtain as follows: Match the bobbin thread to the curtain fabric. Outline the blocks first, matching the needle thread to the appliqué fabric. Stitch the lines separating the blocks, using yellow thread in the needle. Outline the bear's facial features, matching the needle thread to the appliqué fabric, and stitch the highlights, using the colors indicated in **Diagram 7** for the needle thread. Use a longer zigzag stitch for the black eyebrows. Use a narrower zigzag stitch for the red mouth lines and the black line under the nose.

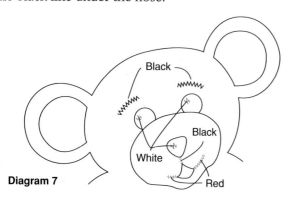

Diagram 7

Referring to **Diagram 8,** outline the inner edges of the paws and the outer edges of the inner ears, using blue thread in the needle. Outline the body and stitch the remaining details, using red thread in the needle. Outline the balloons and the highlights, matching the needle thread to the appliqué fabric. Outline the red balloon first, then the yellow balloon, and then the green balloon. Outline the white highlights last.

Gently tear away the stabilizer.

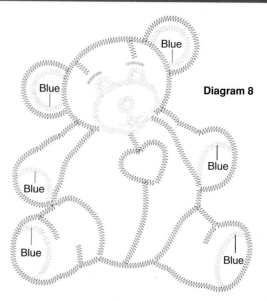

Diagram 8

4 Applying the rickrack and the ribbon

Use the marking pen to draw a line from the bottom of each balloon to the bear's paw. Stitch a piece of baby rickrack in place over each marked line, as shown in the photograph on page 82.

Tie the ribbon in a bow, following the directions on page 128 for tying a bow. Hand sew the bow to the bear's paw, covering the ends of the rickrack.

Use the pen to draw a placement line across the curtain for the yellow maxi-rickrack. Place the line 4″ (10cm) below the bear, as shown in the photo on page 82. Draw a parallel line 4″ (10cm) below the first line for the green maxi-rickrack.

Using the glue stick, baste the yellow maxi-rickrack to the curtain over the first marked line, turning the raw ends under ½″ (1.3cm). Stitch, using two rows of straight stitches, as shown in **Diagram 9.** Repeat, basting and stitching the green maxi-rickrack over the second marked line.

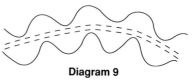

Diagram 9

INSTALLATION

Attach the rod hooks to the shower curtain rod. Hang the liner and the shower curtain on the hooks.

TOWELS & BATH MAT

Size:

Two 26" × 48" (66cm × 122cm) bath towels and one 22" × 30" (56cm × 76cm) bath mat

SUPPLIES

- *Two 26" × 48" (66cm × 122cm) bath towels*
- *One 22" × 30" (56cm × 76cm) bath mat*
- *4" × 12" (10cm × 30.5cm) scraps of red, green, and yellow broadcloth*
- *¼ yard (0.3m) of 18" (45.5cm) wide paper-backed fusible web*
- *3⅝ yards (3.4m) of yellow maxi-rickrack*
- *8" (20.5cm) square of tracing paper (optional)*
- *1 spool each of red, green, yellow, and white machine embroidery thread*
- *½ yard (0.5m) of 22" (56cm) wide tear-away stabilizer*
- *Glue stick*
- *Pencil*

APPLIQUÉ DIRECTIONS

1 Creating the appliqué shapes

Using the tracing paper or a photocopy machine, copy the full-size balloon appliqué pattern shown in **Diagram 1** on page 88.

Using the pencil, trace nine balloon appliqué patterns onto the paper side of the paper-backed fusible web. Cut out each appliqué shape, leaving a small margin of paper-backed fusible web all around the traced outline. Do not remove the paper backings.

Apply three appliqué shapes to the wrong side of each fabric, following the fusible web manufacturer's directions. Cut out each appliqué shape on the traced outline.

2 Fusing the appliqué shapes

Fold one towel in half crosswise; pin mark the fold line. Unfold the towel and refold it in half lengthwise; pin mark the fold line. Unfold the towel. Repeat for the other towel.

Peel off the paper backings and position the appliqué shapes on one towel, using one of each color balloon. Place the yellow balloon along the lengthwise fold line, just below the crosswise fold line. Position a red balloon on one side of the yellow balloon and a green balloon on the other side, forming a cluster, as shown in **Diagram 2.**

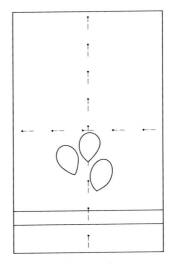

Diagram 2

⊕ DESIGN PLUS

To personalize a towel, use washable, dimensional fabric paint to add the child's name or initials to one of the balloons.

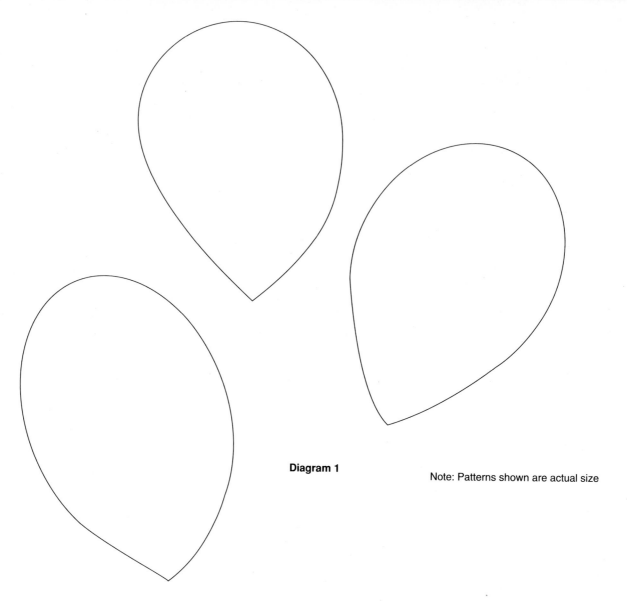

Diagram 1

Note: Patterns shown are actual size

Remove the pins. Fuse the appliqué shapes to the towel, following the fusible web manufacturer's directions. Repeat for the other towel. Repeat for the bath mat, positioning the appliqué shapes at one corner, inside the mat's woven-in band or approximately 6″ (15cm) in from the edges of the mat, as shown in **Diagram 3**.

3 Stitching the appliqué shapes

Cut a piece of tear-away stabilizer that is slightly larger than one balloon cluster. Center the stabilizer over the cluster on the wrong side of one towel. Hand baste it in place.

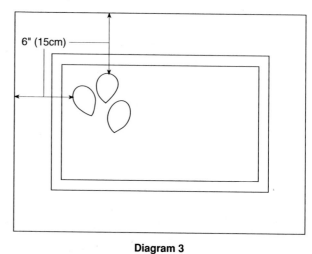

6″ (15cm)

Diagram 3

Using a short, wide machine zigzag stitch and referring to the directions on page 126 for machine appliqué, stitch the shapes to the towel as follows: Match the bobbin thread to the towel. As shown in **Diagram 4,** outline the balloons first and stitch 2″ to 3″ (5cm to 7.5cm) tails, matching the needle thread to the appliqué fabric. Stitch the highlights, using white thread in the needle.

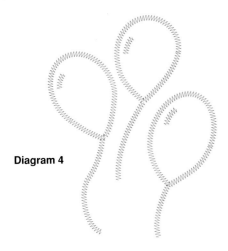

Diagram 4

Repeat for the other towel and the bath mat.

Gently tear away the stabilizer.

🧵 SEW SIMPLE

If your sewing machine has a three-step zigzag stitch, use it instead of two rows of straight stitches to apply the maxi-rickrack.

---

4 Applying the rickrack

Using the glue stick, baste one row of yellow maxi-rickrack across the lower edge of one towel, covering the towel's woven-in band and turning the ends of the rickrack under ½″ (1.3cm). (If there

is no band, position the rickrack approximately 3″ [7.5cm] above the lower edge of the towel.) Stitch, using two rows of straight stitches, as shown in **Diagram 5.**

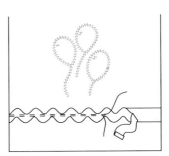

Diagram 5

Repeat, basting and stitching the rickrack to the other towel. Repeat, basting and stitching the rickrack around the bath mat, as shown in **Diagram 6,** covering the mat's woven-in band. (If there is no band, position the rickrack approximately 4″ [10cm] in from the edges.) Conceal the cut ends of the rickrack at one corner, as shown in **Diagram 6.**

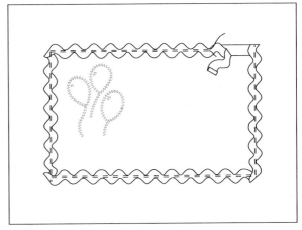

Diagram 6

Ribbons and lace work their special magic on an opulent shower curtain, companion towel, and bath mat.

A FEMININE RETREAT

SHOWER CURTAIN

Size:

72" (183cm) square curtain and 27" (68.5cm) long valance

SUPPLIES

- *7 yards (6.5m) of 54" or 60" (138cm or 153cm) wide decorator fabric, such as chintz, sateen, or polished cotton**
- *½ yard (0.5m) of 54" or 60" (138cm or 153cm) wide contrasting decorator fabric, such as moiré, polished cotton, or taffeta**
- *3⅛ yards (2.9m) of 4" (10cm) wide ruffled lace trim*
- *1 yard (1m) of 2-cord shirring tape*
- *12 large grommets*
- *Plastic shower curtain liner and 12 rod hooks*
- *One 2½" (6.3cm) wide continental rod*
- *1 sheet of tracing paper*
- *Straight-edge ruler and pencil*
- *Safety pins*
- *Water-soluble marking pen*
- *Liquid ravel preventer, such as Fray Check*

*See the "Cutting Directions" for additional information.

CUTTING DIRECTIONS

All measurements include ½" (1.3cm) seam allowances.

Before purchasing printed fabric, review the information on page 124 for working with printed fabrics.

From the decorator fabric, cut:

- *Two 81" (206cm) long curtain panels*
- *One 30" (76cm) long valance center panel*
- *Two 30" (76cm) long valance side panels*

Use the full width of the fabric as the width of each panel.

Split one curtain panel in half lengthwise to form two curtain side panels.

Fold the tracing paper in half. Using the ruler and pencil, measure and mark a half circle with a 5" (12.5cm) radius, as shown in **Diagram 1**. Cut along the marked line. Unfold the paper and use it as a pattern for the 10" (25.5cm) diameter rosettes.

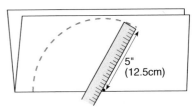

Diagram 1

5" (12.5cm)

From the contrasting decorator fabric, cut:

- *Two 2½" × 54" (6.3cm × 138cm) band sections*
- *Three 10" (25.5cm) diameter rosettes*

SEWING DIRECTIONS

1 Joining the panels

For the shower curtain:

With right sides together, stitch one curtain side panel to each side edge of the curtain center panel, as shown in **Diagram 2.** Press the seams open. Cut an equal amount off each side edge so that the joined panels measure 76" (193cm) wide.

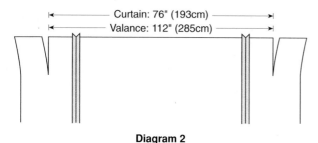

|← Curtain: 76" (193cm) →|
|← Valance: 112" (285cm) →|

Diagram 2

For the valance:

With right sides together, stitch one valance side panel to each side edge of the valance center panel. Press the seams open. Cut an equal amount off each side edge so that the joined panels measure 112" (285cm) wide, as shown in **Diagram 2.**

2 Hemming the panels

For the shower curtain:

Referring to **Diagram 3,** press under 3" (7.5cm) on one side edge of the curtain. Tuck the raw edge in to meet the crease. Press again. Stitch close to the second fold. Repeat for the other side edge and the lower edge of the curtain.

Press under 4" (10cm) on the upper edge of the curtain. Tuck the raw edge in to meet the crease. Press again. Stitch close to the second fold.

For the valance:

Referring again to **Diagram 3,** press under 3" (7.5cm) on one side edge of the valance. Tuck the raw edge in to meet the crease. Press again. Stitch close to the second fold. Repeat for the other side edge.

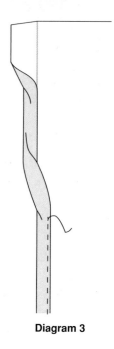

Diagram 3

3 Attaching the grommets

Working on the right side of the curtain, use the marking pen to mark the grommet placement across the top of the curtain, as shown in **Diagram 4.** Place one mark ¾" (2cm) in from each side edge. Place ten more marks at evenly spaced intervals (approximately 6½" [16.5cm] apart) between the first two marks. Place each mark 1" (2.5cm) from the upper edge of the curtain.

Attach one grommet at each mark, following the grommet manufacturer's directions.

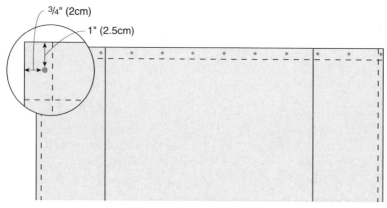

¾" (2cm)

1" (2.5cm)

Diagram 4

SEW SIMPLE

If you prefer, substitute machine buttonholes for the grommets. For durability, stitch twice around each buttonhole. After cutting the buttonholes open, apply liquid ravel preventer to the edges.

4 Making the valance header and rod pocket

Referring to **Diagram 5,** press under 6½″ (16.5cm) along the upper edge of the valance. Press under ½″ (1.3cm) along the raw edge. Stitch close to the second fold. Stitch again 3″ (7.5cm) below the upper edge, creating a 3″ (7.5cm) header and a 3″ (7.5cm) rod pocket.

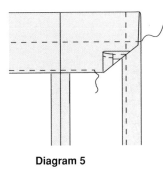

Diagram 5

5 Trimming the valance

With right sides together, stitch the two band sections together at the ends to form one long band, as shown in **Diagram 6.** Press the seam open.

With right sides together, fold the band in half lengthwise. Stitch ½″ (1.3cm) from each end, as shown in **Diagram 7.** Trim the corners on the diagonal. Turn the band right side out. Press.

On the right side of the valance, pin the band to the lower edge of the valance, matching the raw edges of the band to the raw edge of the valance. Machine baste ½″ (1.3cm) from the raw edges, as shown in **Diagram 8.**

Apply liquid ravel preventer to the ends of the ruffled lace trim. Referring to **Diagram 9,** with right sides together, pin the lace trim to the lower edge of the valance over the band, turning the ends of the lace trim to the wrong side. Stitch ½″ (1.3cm) from the lower raw edge of the valance. Machine finish the raw edges. Press the seam allowances toward the valance.

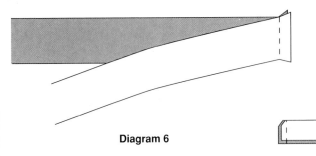

Diagram 6

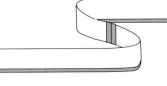

Diagram 7

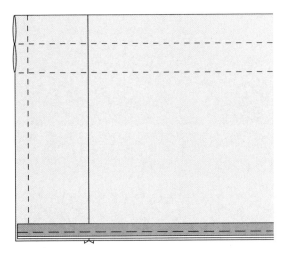

Diagram 8

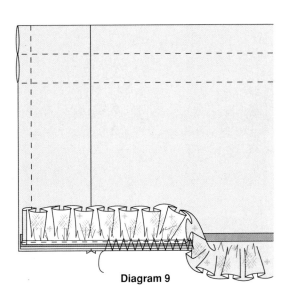

Diagram 9

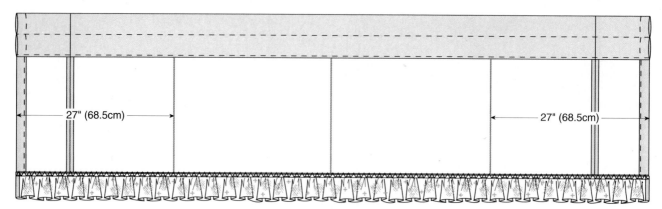

27" (68.5cm)   27" (68.5cm)

Diagram 10

6 Attaching the shirring tape

Working on the wrong side of the valance, use the marking pen to mark the placement of the shirring tape, as shown in **Diagram 10.** With right sides together, fold the valance in half lengthwise. Mark the fold between the header and the lower edge of the valance. Unfold the valance. Measure in 27" (68.5cm) from one side edge and mark a line between the header and the lower edge of the valance. Repeat for the other side edge.

Cut the shirring tape into three equal lengths. Press the ends of each length of shirring tape under 1" (2.5cm). Use a pin to pull out the shirring cords so they are free from the folded ends.

Referring to **Diagram 11,** center one length of shirring tape over each placement line. Stitch each tape in place along both long edges. Do not catch the shirring cords in the stitches.

Knot each pair of shirring cords together at the bottom of the tapes, as shown in **Diagram 12.** Trim the tails close to the knots. Seal the knots with liquid ravel preventer.

Pull up the shirring cords at the top of the center tape until the distance from the bottom of the header to the bottom of the tape is 13" (33cm). Loosely tie the cords together and then wrap them into a loop. Use a safety pin to secure the loop, hiding the pin in the fullness below the header. Repeat for the other two sets of shirring cords.

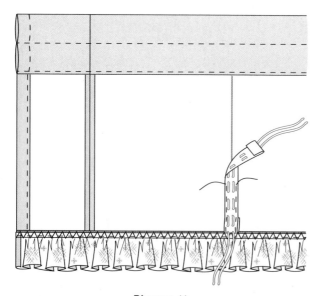

Diagram 11

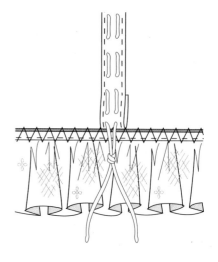

Diagram 12

7 Making the rosettes

Machine baste around the edge of one rosette ½″ (1.3cm) from the raw edge, as shown in **Diagram 13.** Referring to **Diagram 14,** pull up the threads, tucking the raw edges of the rosette in while gathering the fabric. Tie the thread tails together securely. Trim the thread tails. Use liquid ravel preventer to secure the knot. Repeat, making two more rosettes.

Referring to **Diagram 15,** on the right side of the valance, pin one rosette in place at the bottom of one row of shirring tape, so that the gathered back of the rosette is approximately 2″ (5cm) above the lace edging. Hand sew the back of the rosette to the valance. Referring to **Diagram 16,** shape the rosette by pushing the fabric down into the center, creating soft folds. Use hand stitches to tack the folds in place at the center of the rosette. Repeat, attaching and shaping the other two rosettes.

INSTALLATION

Install the continental rod slightly above the shower curtain rod.

Attach the rod hooks to the shower curtain rod. Hang the liner and the shower curtain on the hooks. Hang the valance on the continental rod, as shown in the photograph on page 90.

⊕ DESIGN PLUS

For a different look, match the band and the rosettes to the shower curtain. Use a contrasting fabric for the valance. To do this, you'll need 5 yards (4.6m) of decorator fabric and 2½ yards (2.3m) of contrasting fabric.

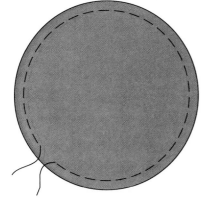

Diagram 13

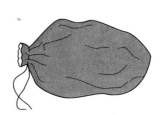

Diagram 14

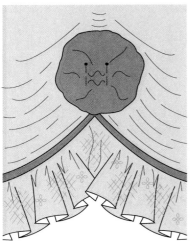

Diagram 15

Diagram 16

TOWEL & BATH MAT

Size:

One 26" × 48" (66cm × 122cm) bath towel
and one 22" × 30" (56cm × 76cm) bath mat

SUPPLIES

- *One 26" × 48" (66cm × 122cm) bath towel*
- *One 22" × 30" (56cm × 76cm) bath mat*
- *5½ yards (5.1m) of ¾" (2cm) wide white lace beading*
- *5½ yards (5.1m) of ¼" (7mm) wide light blue satin ribbon*
- *28" (71cm) of ⅞" (23mm) wide light blue satin ribbon*
- *18" (45.5cm) of 1½" (39mm) wide light blue satin ribbon*
- *28" (71cm) of 4" (10cm) wide white ruffled lace trim*
- *3 large pearl beads*
- *1 spool of light blue heavy-duty thread*
- *Glue stick*

CUTTING DIRECTIONS

Weave the ¼" (7mm) wide ribbon through the lace
beading and then cut:

- *Two 28" (71cm) lengths of beading for the towel*
- *Two 34" (86.5cm) lengths and two 24" (61cm) lengths of beading for the bath mat*

SEWING DIRECTIONS

1 Trimming the towel

Referring to **Diagram 1,** assemble the trim band.
Lap one 28" (71cm) length of beading slightly over
one edge of the ⅞" (23mm) wide satin ribbon and
stitch. Repeat for the other edge of the ribbon.
Lap one beading edge over the top of the lace trim
and stitch.

Diagram 1

🧵 SEW SIMPLE

*Use a nonwoven tear-away stabilizer, such as
Stitch-N-Tear, underneath the trims to provide
support when assembling the band. Tear off the
stabilizer before basting and stitching the band
to the towel.*

Using the glue stick, baste the trim band to the towel so that the lower edge of the lace trim is aligned with the lower edge of the towel. Stitch the band to the towel along the upper edge of the top row of beading.

Referring to **Diagram 2,** fold one end of the band under ½" (1.3cm) and wrap it around to the wrong side of the towel. Stitch along the fold and again at the edge of the towel, stitching through the ribbon, the beading, and the towel. Repeat for the other end of the band.

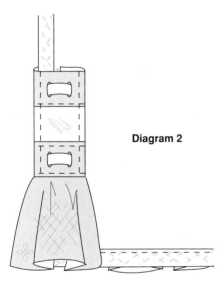

Diagram 2

2 Trimming the bath mat

Using the glue stick, baste one 34" (86.5cm) length of beading parallel to one long edge of the mat 4" (10cm) in from the edge or covering the mat's woven-in band. Fold the ends of the beading under ½" (1.3cm) and wrap them around to the wrong side of the mat. Stitch along both long edges of the beading, catching the folded-under ends in the stitching. Repeat, applying the other 34" (86.5cm)

length of beading parallel to the other long edge and applying the 24" (61cm) lengths of beading parallel to the side edges, as shown in **Diagram 3.**

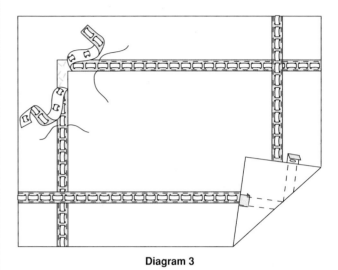

Diagram 3

3 Adding the bows

Cut the 1½" (39mm) wide ribbon into three equal lengths.

Referring to **Diagram 4,** fold one ribbon length crosswise into thirds. String a pearl onto a 20" (51cm) long piece of heavy-duty thread. Position the pearl at the center of the folded ribbon and wrap the thread tails around the ribbon several times, pulling it tight to form a bow. Tie the thread tails in a knot at the back of the bow. Clip the tails. Repeat, making two more bows.

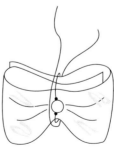

Diagram 4

Referring to the photograph on page 90, sew one bow at the center of the towel band. Sew the remaining bows to the beading at diagonally opposite corners of the mat.

*F*or *an extra-special touch, choose this eye-catching*
shower curtain with pinch-pleat tabs.

SHOWER POWER

Size:

72" (183cm) square

SUPPLIES

- $7^{1}/8$ yards (6.6m) of 45" (115cm) wide or $4^{3}/4$ yards (4.4m) of 60" (153cm) wide decorator fabric, such as broadcloth, chintz, sateen, or polished cotton*
- Plastic shower curtain liner and 12 rod hooks
- Tracing paper
- Shirt cardboard
- Pencil
- Water-soluble marking pen

*See the "Cutting Directions" for additional information.

CUTTING DIRECTIONS

All measurements include $1/2$" (1.3cm) seam allowances.

Before purchasing printed fabric, review the information on page 124 for working with printed fabrics.

From the decorator fabric, cut the shower curtain panels. The width of the fabric determines the number of panels.

- From 45" (115cm) wide fabric, cut three 45" (115cm) wide × $84^{1}/2$" (215cm) long panels for the center panel and two side panels.
- From 60" (153cm) wide fabric, cut one 60" (153cm) wide × $84^{1}/2$" (215cm) long panel. Split the remaining fabric in half and cut two 30" (76cm) wide × $84^{1}/2$" (215cm) long side panels.

SEWING DIRECTIONS

1 Joining the panels

With right sides together, stitch one side panel to each side edge of the center panel, as shown in **Diagram 1.** Press the seams open. Cut an equal amount off each side edge so that the joined panels measure $110^{1}/2$" (281cm) wide.

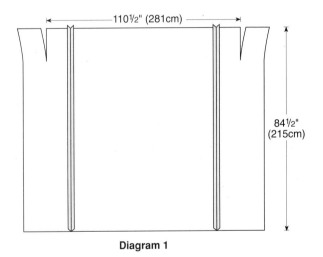

Diagram 1

2 Hemming the curtain

Referring to **Diagram 2,** press under 2″ (5cm) on one side edge. Tuck the raw edge in to meet the crease. Press again. Stitch close to the second fold. Repeat for the other side edge.

Press under 8″ (20.5cm) on the lower edge. Tuck the raw edge in to meet the crease. Press again. Stitch close to the second fold.

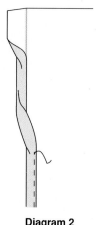

Diagram 2

3 Making the template

Use tracing paper and a pencil to trace the full-size scallop pattern shown in **Diagram 3.** Cut out the pattern and trace it onto the shirt cardboard. Cut out the scallop template.

4 Stitching the header

Press under ½″ (1.3cm) on the upper edge of the curtain.

With wrong sides together, fold the curtain in half lengthwise. Use the marking pen to mark the center fold of the curtain, starting at the upper edge and ending about 12″ (30.5cm) from that edge. Unfold the curtain.

Referring to **Diagram 4,** with right sides together, fold the upper edge of the curtain down 4″ (10cm). Pin the layers together but do not press.

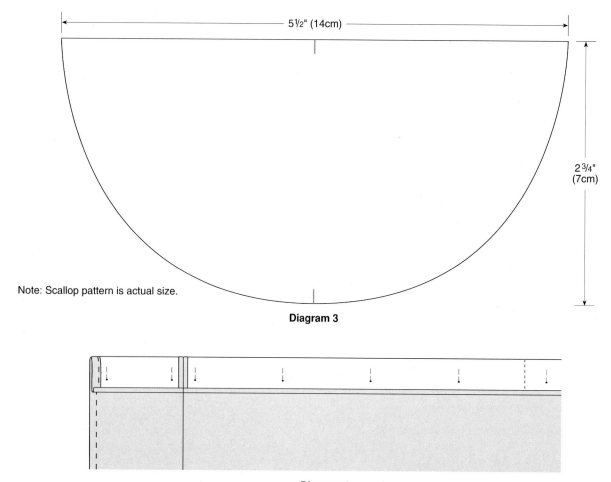

5½″ (14cm)

2³⁄₄″ (7cm)

Note: Scallop pattern is actual size.

Diagram 3

Diagram 4

Center the template on the upper edge of the curtain, as shown in **Diagram 5,** matching the straight edge of the template to the folded edge of the curtain. Use the marking pen to trace the curved edge.

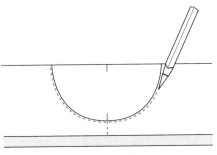

Diagram 5

Working from the center out to one side edge, trace five more scallops, spacing the scallops 4″ (10cm) apart, as shown in **Diagram 6.** Repeat, working from the center out to the other side edge. If necessary, reposition the pins so that they do not cross the scallop markings.

Referring to **Diagram 7,** stitch the layers together along the traced scallops. Backstitch at the beginning and end of each scallop, following the directions on page 124 for backstitching.

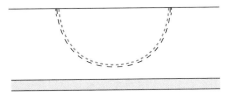

Diagram 7

Cut away the fabric inside each scallop, leaving ¼″ (6mm) seam allowances, and clip the curves, as shown in **Diagram 8.**

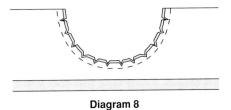

Diagram 8

Remove the pins. Turn the header right side out. Press. Stitch across the lower edge of the header, as shown in **Diagram 9.**

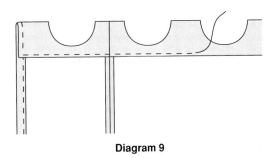

Diagram 9

✦ DESIGN PLUS

To add a coordinating border, stitch ⅞″ (23mm) wide ribbon along the sides and lower edge of the curtain before pleating the header.

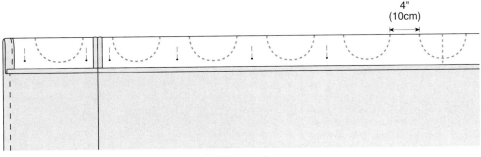

4″
(10cm)

Diagram 6

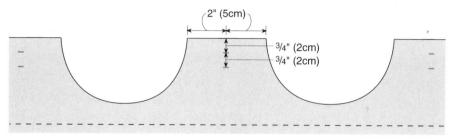

Diagram 10

5 Making the hook openings

Referring to **Diagram 10,** use the marking pen to mark the placement of the hook openings. Mark the center of each tab ¾" (2cm) from the upper edge of the curtain. Mark again ¾" (2cm) below the first marks.

Make one ¾" (2cm) long machine buttonhole between each set of marks, as shown in **Diagram 11.**

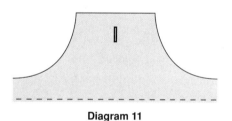

Diagram 11

6 Pleating the header

Referring to **Diagram 12,** fold the header right sides together along one hook opening. Fold the header back on itself, matching the sides of the tab to the first fold and forming an accordion pleat. Pin the layers together to keep the upper edges even and then stitch across the base of the pleats 2" (5cm) from the upper edge of the header. Remove the pins.

Repeat, making 11 more sets of pleats.

INSTALLATION

Attach the rod hooks to the shower curtain rod. Hang the liner and the shower curtain on the hooks.

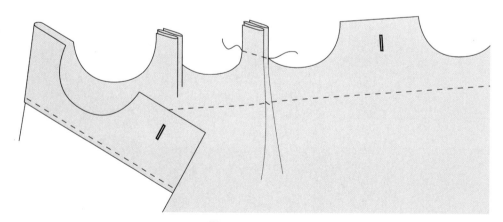

Diagram 12

HOLD IT!

Make an everyday wastebasket special with a fabric slipcover that's both practical and pretty.

WASTE LINE

Size:

To fit a 10″ to 13″ (25.5cm to 33cm) tall × 10″ to 12″ (25.5cm to 30.5cm) diameter wastebasket

SUPPLIES

- *One 10″ to 13″ (25.5cm to 33cm) tall × 10″ to 12″ (25.5cm to 30.5cm) diameter wastebasket*
- *1¼ yards (1.2m) of 45″ (115cm) wide decorator fabric, such as broadcloth, dotted swiss, polished cotton, or batiste*
- *2½ yards (2.3m) of 3¼″ (8.3cm) wide flat eyelet trim*
- *⅞ yards (0.9m) of ¼″ (6mm) wide elastic*
- *Bodkin or safety pin*
- *Double-faced carpet tape*
- *Tissue paper*
- *Pencil*

CUTTING DIRECTIONS

Make a pattern for the base by tracing the bottom of the wastebasket onto the tissue paper. Add ½″ (1.3cm) all around for the seam allowance.

From the decorator fabric and using the paper pattern, cut:

- *1 base*
- *Two 15″ × 45″ (38cm × 115cm) panels*

SEWING DIRECTIONS

1 Assembling the panels

With right sides together, stitch the short ends of the panels together with ½″ (1.3cm) seams to make one continuous panel. Press the seams open.

2 Making the hem and casing

Press under ½″ (1.3cm) along the upper edge of the panel. Press under again 2″ (5cm).

With right sides together, pin the eyelet to the upper edge of the panel, matching the lower edge of the eyelet to the lower edge of the hem allowance and pressing the ends of the eyelet under, as shown in **Diagram 1.**

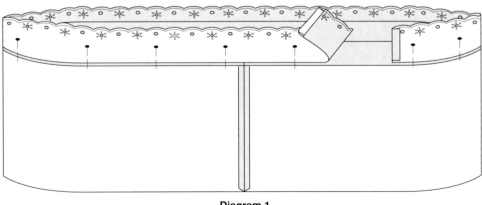

Diagram 1

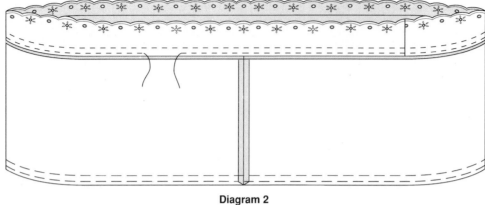

Diagram 2

Referring to **Diagram 2,** stitch along the lower edge of the eyelet, through all of the layers, leaving a 1″ (2.5cm) opening for inserting the elastic. Stitch again ⅜″ (1cm) above the first stitching, through all of the layers. Machine baste ½″ (1.3cm) and 1″ (2.5cm) from the lower edge of the panel.

3 Attaching the base

Divide and mark the lower edge of the panel and the edge of the base into four equal parts. Pin the panel to the base, with right sides together and marks matching. Pull up the basting stitches, gathering the panel to fit the base. Adjust the gathers to distribute the fullness evenly. Stitch all around the base, ½″ (1.3cm) from the raw edges, and press the seam toward the base, as shown in **Diagram 3.** Remove the basting stitches.

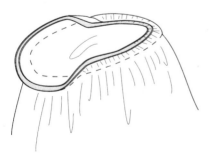

Diagram 3

4 Inserting the elastic

Attach the bodkin or safety pin to one end of the elastic and pull it through the casing. Referring to **Diagram 4,** overlap the ends of the elastic and stitch them together securely. Stretch the cover until the ends of the elastic retract into the casing.

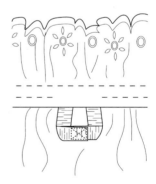

Diagram 4

🧵 SEW SIMPLE

Before making the hem, use 2″ (5cm) long strips of fusible web to secure the seam allowances at the top of the panel. When the elastic is inserted, the bodkin or safety pin will glide smoothly over the seam allowances.

INSTALLATION

Slide the cover over the wastebasket. Use the pencil to mark the location of the casing on the wastebasket. Remove the cover. Wrap carpet tape around the wastebasket at the casing level. Slide the cover over the wastebasket and press the casing in place over the tape.

⊕ DESIGN PLUS

For a softer, more romantic look, cut two 15" × 45" (38cm × 115cm) panels from a delicate lace fabric and two 15" × 45" (38cm × 115cm) underlining panels from a soft broadcloth or batiste. Baste the lace panels to the underlining panels, with the wrong side of the lace matching the right side of the underlining. Use a sturdy decorator fabric, such as polished cotton, in a coordinating color for the base. If desired, decorate the finished cover with purchased bows and ribbon roses.

Ribbon and rickrack adorn a no-sew tissue box cover-up that's whimsical as well as practical.

BOXED IN

Size:

4¾″ (12cm) square × 5¼″ (13.5cm) tall box

SUPPLIES

- ¼ *yard (0.3m) of 45″ (115cm) wide decorator fabric, such as chintz or polished cotton*
- ⅝ *yard (0.6m) of medium rickrack*
- 1½ *yards (1.4m) of ⅜″ (9mm) wide satin ribbon*
- *One 6″ × 28″ (15cm × 71cm) piece of corrugated cardboard*
- *Craft knife*
- *Clear-drying craft glue*
- *1 empty boutique-size tissue box*
- *1 full box of boutique-size tissues*
- *Push pins*

CUTTING DIRECTIONS

From the cardboard and using the craft knife, cut:

- *Four 4¾″ × 5¼″ (12cm × 13.5cm) base sections*
- *One 4¾″ (12cm) square lid*

Open the empty tissue box. Center the top of the box on the cardboard lid; trace the oval opening. Use the craft knife to cut out the opening along the traced line, as shown in **Diagram 1.**

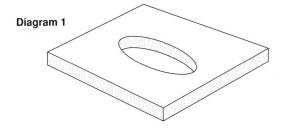

Diagram 1

From the decorator fabric, cut:

- *One 7¼″ × 20″ (18.5cm × 51cm) cover*
- *One 5¼″ (13.5cm) square top*

ASSEMBLY DIRECTIONS

1 Constructing the base

Glue the base sections together along the 5¼″ (13.5cm) edges, forming a box with open ends, as shown in **Diagram 2.** Let the glue dry thoroughly.

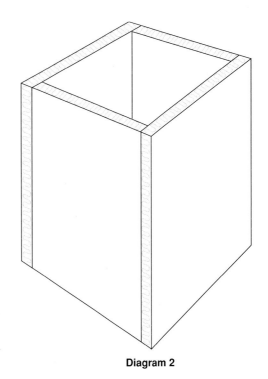

Diagram 2

2 Covering the base

Referring to **Diagram 3,** position the cover right side up on the box so that there is a ½" (1.3cm) underlap at one side edge and a 1" (2.5cm) margin of fabric at the upper and lower edges. Use push pins to temporarily secure the cover. Glue the cover in place, starting at one corner of the underlap and working around the base. At the overlap, fold the fabric under so that the edge of the overlap just meets the side edge of the base. Fold and glue the excess fabric at the upper and lower edges to the inside of the base.

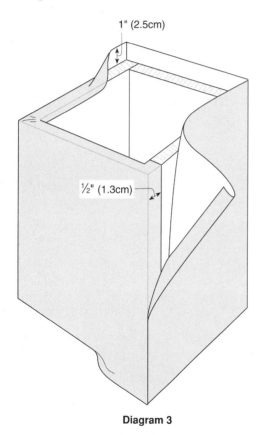

1" (2.5cm)

½" (1.3cm)

Diagram 3

⊛ DESIGN PLUS

For an upholstered look, glue polyester batting to the cardboard box and lid before covering them with fabric. Use narrow, twisted cord in place of the rickrack and add a small tassel at the center of the bow.

3 Covering the lid

Referring to **Diagram 4,** center the top over the lid and glue it in place. Wrap and glue the excess fabric to the underside of the lid. Turn the lid wrong side up and snip a small hole in the center of the oval opening. Make several clips in the fabric, from the hole to the edge of the opening. Wrap and glue the fabric to the inside of the lid.

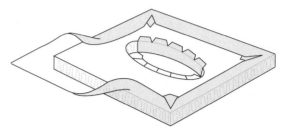

Diagram 4

4 Finishing the cover

Glue the lid to the top of the base. Glue rickrack around the outer edges of the lid and around the edge of the opening, as shown in **Diagram 5.**

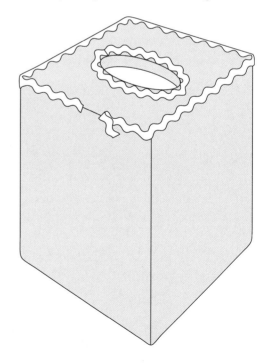

Diagram 5

Starting approximately 6″ (15cm) from one end of the ribbon, loop the ribbon back and forth to form three 5″ (12.5cm) long loops, as shown in **Diagram 6.** Tie the loops and tails together in a half-knot, as shown in **Diagram 7.** Glue the triple bow in place on the cover and trim the tails on the diagonal, as shown in the photograph on page 108.

Slide the cover in place over the full box of boutique-size tissues.

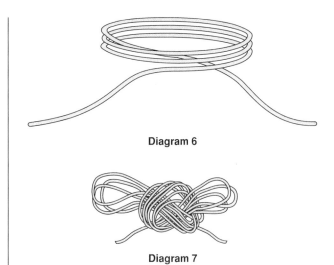

Diagram 6

Diagram 7

Pamper yourself or favor a friend with a
fabric-covered basket filled to the brim with
some of life's little pleasures.

A TISKET, A TASKET

Size:

To fit any size basket

SUPPLIES

- *Round or oval basket with handle*
- *45" to 54" (115cm to 138cm) wide decorator fabric, such as broadcloth, chintz, dotted swiss, or batiste**
- *2¼" (5.7cm) wide ruffled eyelet trim**
- *Polyester batting**
- *⅜" (1cm) wide elastic**
- *3 to 4 yards (2.8m to 3.7m) of medium rickrack*
- *3 yards (2.8m) of ³⁄₁₆" (5mm) wide satin ribbon*
- *1½ yards (1.4m) of ⅝" (15mm) wide satin ribbon*
- *Craft glue*
- *Brown paper**
- *Pencil*
- *Tape measure*
- *Water-soluble marking pen*
- *Bodkin or small safety pin*

*See the "Cutting Directions" for additional information.

CUTTING DIRECTIONS

Measure the height of the basket and the circumference at the upper edge, as shown in **Diagram 1.**

Purchase a length of ⅜" (1cm) wide elastic equal to the circumference of the basket minus 1" (2.5cm).

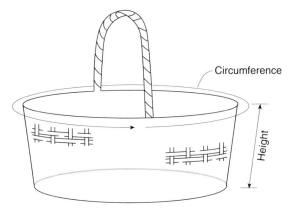

Diagram 1

Place the basket in the center of a large piece of brown paper. Trace around the bottom of the basket. Remove the basket.

Referring to **Diagram 2,** measure out from the traced line a distance equal to the height of the basket and mark all around. This is the cutting line for the batting. Measure out again 3" (7.5cm) from the second line and mark all around. This is the cutting line for the cover and the lining.

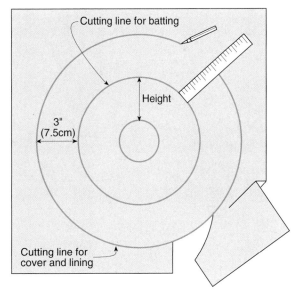

Diagram 2

Use the paper pattern and the following cutting directions to determine how much decorator fabric and batting to purchase. Purchase enough eyelet trim to equal the distance around the outer edge of the paper pattern plus 2″ (5cm).

From the decorator fabric and using the paper pattern, cut one cover and one cover lining.

From the batting and using the paper pattern, cut two pieces of batting.

SEWING DIRECTIONS

1 Assembling the cover

Use the marking pen to mark a seam line ½″ (1.3cm) from the raw edge on the right side of the cover. Mark all around the cover. Pin the eyelet trim to the cover, with right sides together and the straight edge of the trim within the seam allowance. Turn the ends of the trim under and overlap them. Machine baste the trim to the cover along the seam line.

Referring to **Diagram 3** and with right sides together, pin the cover to the lining. Stitch along the seam line, all around the cover. Clip the curves. Cut a 3″ to 4″ (7.5cm to 10cm) slash in the center of the lining for turning. Do not cut the cover. Turn the cover right side out through the opening. Press.

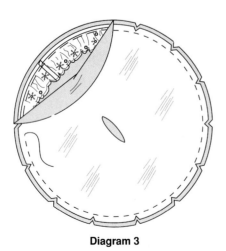

Diagram 3

> ### 🧵 SEW SIMPLE
>
> *Waterproof the outside of the basket with a layer of Heat n Bond iron-on flexible vinyl. Apply it to the right side of the cover, following the flexible vinyl manufacturer's directions, before basting the eyelet trim in place.*

2 Making the casing

Stitch all around the cover 2″ (5cm) from the edge of the cover. Stitch again 2½″ (6.3cm) from the edge of the cover, as shown in **Diagram 4.**

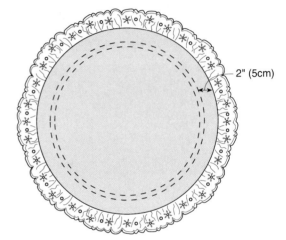

2″ (5cm)

Diagram 4

Cut a small opening in the lining between the two rows of stitches. Attach the bodkin or small safety pin to one end of the elastic. Referring to **Diagram 5,** thread the elastic through the casing, overlap the ends, and stitch them together securely. Stretch the cover until the ends of the elastic retract into the casing.

Diagram 5

3 Padding the basket

Place the batting sections together, raw edges matching, on a flat surface. Place the basket in the center. Bring the edges of the batting up around the basket and glue them in place, easing in the fullness, as shown in **Diagram 6.**

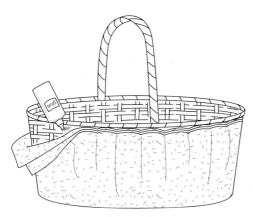

Diagram 6

4 Finishing the basket

Slide the cover over the basket.

Wrap and glue two lengths of rickrack around the handle, as shown in the photograph on page 112. Cut the remaining rickrack into three equal lengths.

Cut the $\frac{3}{16}''$ (5mm) wide ribbon into two equal lengths. Tie each length into a small four-loop bow, following the directions on page 128 for tying a bow. Tie the $\frac{5}{8}''$ (15mm) wide ribbon into a large four-loop bow.

Referring to the photograph on page 112, glue the large bow, one small bow, and the lengths of rickrack to the handle. Glue the other small bow to the front of the cover.

⊕ DESIGN PLUS

This versatile basket is perfect for bearing special gifts. Choose springtime colors and fill it with Easter goodies; choose Valentine prints and fill it with chocolate kisses. If desired, spray paint the basket to coordinate with the fabrics and trims.

K*eepsake boxes provide stylish resting places for everything from trinkets to treasures.*

VICTORIAN BOXES

ROUND BOXES

Sizes:

8" (20.5cm) diameter × 5½" (14cm) deep small box;
12" (30.5cm) diameter × 7" (18cm) deep large box

SUPPLIES

- *Metal ruler*
- *Compass*
- *Pencil*
- *Craft knife*
- *Clear-drying craft glue*
- *Water*
- *Paintbrush*
- *Hot-glue gun and glue sticks*
- *18-gauge wire*

SMALL BOX

- *One 16" × 27" (40.5cm × 68.5cm) piece of posterboard*
- *⅝ yard (0.6m) of 45" to 60" (115cm to 153cm) wide decorator fabric, such as broadcloth, calico, chintz, or synthetic suede*
- *⅝ yard (0.6m) of 45" to 60" (115cm to 153cm) wide lining fabric*
- *One 8" (20.5cm) square of polyester batting*
- *1½ yards (1.4m) of 18" (45.5cm) wide paper-backed fusible web*

- *1½ yards (1.4m) of 1½" (39mm) wide satin ribbon*
- *1 yard (1m) each of two colors of ¼" (7mm) wide satin ribbon*
- *1 small bouquet of silk flowers*

LARGE BOX

- *One 22" × 40" (56cm × 102cm) piece of posterboard*
- *1 yard (1m) of 45" to 60" (115cm to 153cm) wide decorator fabric, such as broadcloth, calico, chintz, or synthetic suede*
- *1 yard (1m) of 45" to 60" (115cm to 153cm) wide lining fabric*
- *One 12" (30.5cm) square of polyester batting*
- *3⅜ yards (3.1m) of 18" (45.5cm) wide paper-backed fusible web*
- *One 9" × 13" (23cm × 33cm) piece each of nylon netting and contrasting decorator fabric*
- *1 small bouquet of silk flowers*
- *Needle and thread*

CUTTING DIRECTIONS

For the small box:

On the posterboard, use the ruler, compass, and pencil to draw:

- *One 8" (20.5cm) diameter lid*
- *One 1½" × 26" (3.8cm × 66cm) lip*
- *One 7¾" (19.5cm) diameter bottom*
- *One 5½" × 25½" (14cm × 65cm) side*

On the paper side of the fusible web, use the ruler, compass, and pencil to draw:

- *One 10" (25.5cm) diameter lid cover*
- *One 3½" × 27" (9cm × 68.5cm) lip cover*
- *One 9¾" (25cm) diameter bottom cover*
- *One 7½" × 26½" (19cm × 67.5cm) side cover*

For the large box:

On the posterboard, use the ruler, compass, and pencil to draw:

- *One 12" (30.5cm) diameter lid*
- *One 1½" × 39" (3.8cm × 99cm) lip*
- *One 11¾" (30cm) diameter bottom*
- *One 7" × 38¾" (18cm × 98.5cm) side*

On the paper side of the fusible web, use the ruler, compass, and pencil to draw:

- *One 14" (35.5cm) diameter lid cover*
- *One 3½" × 40" (9cm × 102cm) lip cover*
- *One 13¾" (35cm) diameter bottom cover*
- *One 9" × 39¾" (23cm × 101cm) side cover*

For all boxes:

Use the craft knife to score the posterboard along the pencil lines. Cut out the shapes along the scored lines. Use the metal ruler to guide the knife when cutting the straight sections.

Cut out the fusible web shapes, leaving a ½" (1.3cm) margin of paper-backed fusible web around each shape. Apply the shapes to the wrong side of the decorator fabric, following the fusible web manufacturer's directions. Cut out the cover sections along the traced lines. Leave the paper backing in place.

Trace the posterboard lid, lip, bottom, and side shapes onto the paper side of the fusible web. Space the shapes about 1" (2.5cm) apart. Cut out the shapes, leaving a ½" (1.3cm) margin of fusible web around each. Apply the fusible web shapes to the wrong side of the lining fabric, following the fusible web manufacturer's directions. Cut out the lining sections, cutting ⅛" (3mm) inside the traced lines. Leave the paper backing in place.

ASSEMBLY DIRECTIONS

1 Padding the lid

Trace the posterboard lid onto the batting. Cut out one lid batting.

Dilute a small amount of craft glue with water. Brush the glue onto the posterboard lid. Gently press the batting in place on the lid. Let the glue dry.

2 Covering the lid and the bottom

Place the lid cover wrong side up on a flat surface. Peel off the paper. Center the posterboard lid, batting side down, on top of the cover. Cut small wedges from the excess fabric to reduce bulk, as shown in **Diagram 1.** Wrap the excess fabric over the edge of the posterboard and fuse in place, as shown in **Diagram 2** and following the fusible web manufacturer's directions.

Peel off the paper on the lid lining. Center the lid lining, fusible side down, over the wrong side of the lid, as shown in **Diagram 3.** Fuse the lining in place, following the fusible web manufacturer's directions. Turn the lid over and fuse the cover to the batting.

Repeat, covering the unpadded posterboard bottom with the corresponding cover and lining sections.

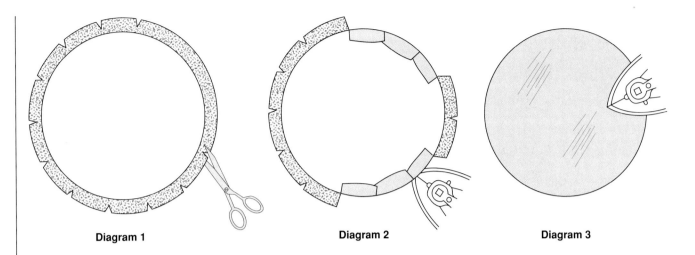

Diagram 1   Diagram 2   Diagram 3

3 Covering the lip and the side

Place the lip cover, wrong side up, on a flat surface. Peel off the paper. Center the posterboard lip on top of the cover. Trim the fabric on the diagonal at the corners, as shown in **Diagram 4.** Wrap the excess fabric over the edges of the posterboard and fuse in place, following the fusible web manufacturer's directions.

Diagram 4

Peel off the paper on the lip lining. Center the lip lining, fusible side down, over the wrong side of the lip. Fuse the lining in place, following the fusible web manufacturer's directions. Turn the lip over and fuse the cover to the posterboard.

Repeat, covering the posterboard side with the corresponding cover and lining sections.

4 Attaching the lip and the side

Place the lid, cover side down, on a flat surface. Wrap the lip around the outer edge of the lid and mark where the ends overlap, as shown in **Diagram 5.** Remove the lip. Overlap the lip ends and hot-glue them together. Hot-glue the lip to the lid, working from the inside of the lid, as shown in **Diagram 6.**

5 Decorating the lid

For the small box:

Referring to **Diagram 7,** make a small loop at one end of the 1½″ (39mm) wide ribbon. Fold the ribbon back and forth under the small loop to form two 3″ (7.5mm) loops. Make two more sets of 3″ (7.5mm) loops, placing each set of loops on a diagonal to the first set, as shown in **Diagram 8.**

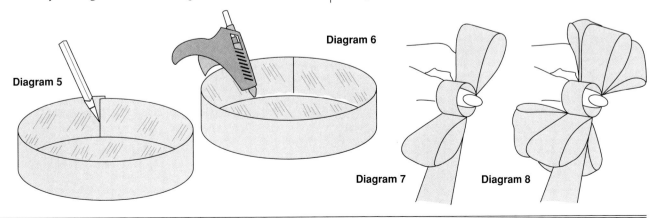

Diagram 5   Diagram 6   Diagram 7   Diagram 8

Bring the end of the ribbon under the bow to form a loop. Use the 18-gauge wire to fasten all of the loops together, as shown in **Diagram 9.** Cut the bottom loop in half to form two tails. Notch the tails.

Diagram 9

Cut each yard (meter) of ¼″ (7mm) wide ribbon into two lengths. Wrap the lengths together around the stems of the bouquet and tie them in a bow, following the directions on page 128 for tying a bow. Trim the tails on the diagonal.

Hot-glue the large bow in place at the center of the lid. Hot-glue the bouquet in place on top of the bow.

For the large box:

Referring to **Diagram 10,** fold the netting in half lengthwise. Hand baste the layers together at the long edge. Draw up the stitches, gathering

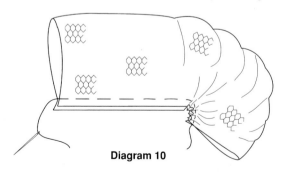

Diagram 10

the netting. Knot the thread to secure. Fold the contrasting decorator fabric in half lengthwise, with wrong sides together, so that the long raw edges overlap slightly at the center, as shown in **Diagram 11.** Hot-glue the edges together.

Diagram 11

Fold the fabric in half crosswise so that the ends overlap slightly at the center. Wrap the 18-gauge wire tightly around the center of the fabric, shaping the fabric into a bow, as shown in **Diagram 12.**

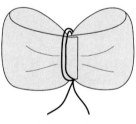

Diagram 12

Hot-glue the netting, bow, and bouquet in place at the center of the lid, as shown in the photograph on page 116.

⊕ DESIGN PLUS

For a Midas touch, cover your box in a metallic print. Decorate the lid with beads, gemstones, tassels, and glittery ribbons.

RECTANGULAR BOX

Size:

6″ × 8″ (15cm × 20.5cm) × 5″ (12.5cm) deep box

SUPPLIES

- One *18″ × 25″ (45.5cm × 63.5cm) piece of cardboard, such as chipboard or bristol board*
- One *21″ × 23″ (53.5cm × 58.5cm) piece of decorator fabric, such as broadcloth, calico, chintz, or synthetic suede*
- One *11¼″ × 13¼″ (28.5cm × 33.5cm) piece of contrasting decorator fabric*
- *½ yard (0.5m) of 45″ (115cm) wide lining fabric*
- One *7¼″ × 9¼″ (18.5cm × 23.5cm) piece of polyester batting*
- *1⅜ yards (1.3m) of 18″ (45.5cm) wide paper-backed fusible web*
- *1″ (2.5cm) wide paper tape*
- *Clear-drying craft glue*
- *Water*
- *Paintbrush*
- *Craft knife*
- *Metal ruler*
- *Pencil*
- *Push pins*

CUTTING DIRECTIONS

On the cardboard, use the ruler and pencil to draw:

- One *8¼″ × 10¼″ (21cm × 26cm) lid*
- One *15″ × 17″ (38cm × 43cm) box*

Use the craft knife to score the cardboard along the pencil lines. Cut out the shapes along the

scored lines. Use the metal ruler to guide the knife when cutting the straight sections. Cut off a 1″ (2.5cm) square at each corner of the lid and a 4½″ (11.5cm) square at each corner of the box, as shown in **Diagram 1.**

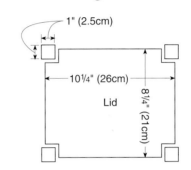

1″ (2.5cm)

10¼″ (26cm)

8¼″ (21cm)

Lid

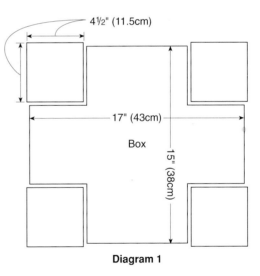

4½″ (11.5cm)

17″ (43cm)

Box

15″ (38cm)

Diagram 1

Referring to **Diagram 2** on page 122 and spacing the shapes about 1″ (2.5cm) apart, on the paper side of the fusible web, draw:

- *1 lid cover by tracing the cardboard lid shape and then drawing new cutting lines 1″ (2.5cm) outside the traced lines.*
- *1 box cover by tracing the cardboard box shape and then drawing new cutting lines 1″ (2.5cm) outside the traced lines.*

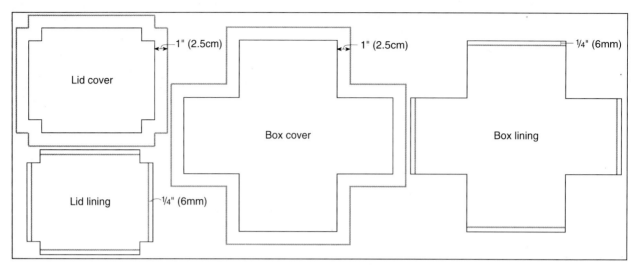

Diagram 2

- *1 lid lining by tracing the cardboard lid shape and then drawing new cutting lines ¼" (6mm) inside the traced lines at the outer edges of the shape.*

- *1 box lining by tracing the cardboard box shape and then drawing new cutting lines ¼" (6mm) inside the traced lines at the outer edges of the shape.*

Cut out the fusible web shapes, leaving a ½" (1.3cm) margin of paper-backed fusible web around each shape.

Apply the fusible web box cover shape to the wrong side of the decorator fabric, following the fusible web manufacturer's directions. Repeat, applying the fusible web lid cover shape to the wrong side of the contrasting decorator fabric. Cut out the cover sections. Leave the paper backing in place.

Apply the box lining and the lid lining fusible web shapes to the wrong side of the lining fabric, following the fusible web manufacturer's directions. Cut out the lining sections. Leave the paper backing in place.

ASSEMBLY DIRECTIONS

1 Shaping the box and the lid

Use the craft knife and metal ruler to score the cardboard lid between each set of cutout corners, as shown in **Diagram 3.**

Place the lid, scored side up, on a table, aligning one scored line with the table edge, as shown in **Diagram 4.** Fold the lid down along the scored

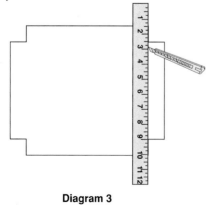

Diagram 3

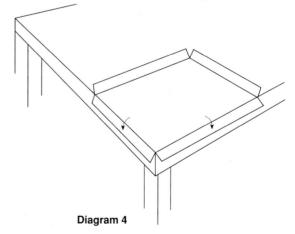

Diagram 4

line, pressing the side of the lid against the side of the table. Repeat, shaping the other three sides of the lid.

Repeat for the cardboard box, shaping the four sides of the box.

Referring to **Diagram 5,** use paper tape to secure each corner of the lid. Repeat, securing each corner of the box.

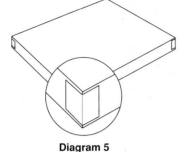

Diagram 5

2 Padding the lid

Dilute a small amount of craft glue with water. Brush the glue onto the top of the cardboard lid. Center the batting on the lid and gently press it in place. Let the glue dry.

3 Covering the lid and the box

Place the lid cover, wrong side up, on a flat surface. Peel off the paper. Center the cardboard lid, batting side down, on top of the cover. Trim the fabric at each corner, as shown in **Diagram 6.**

Referring to **Diagram 7,** wrap and fuse the cover to the 8" (20.5cm) sides of the lid, wrapping the

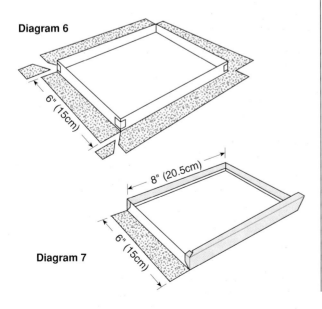

Diagram 6

8" (20.5cm)

6" (15cm)

Diagram 7

cover over the edge of the lid and fusing, following the fusible web manufacturer's directions. Repeat, wrapping and fusing the cover to the 6" (15cm) sides.

Turn the lid over and fuse the cover to the top of the lid.

Repeat, fusing the box cover to the cardboard box.

4 Applying the linings

Peel the paper off the lid lining.

Referring to **Diagram 8,** center the lining, fusible side down, on the inside of the lid. Fuse the lining to the inside top and the 8" (20.5cm) sides, following the fusible web manufacturer's directions. Repeat, fusing the lining to the 6" (15cm) sides.

Diagram 8

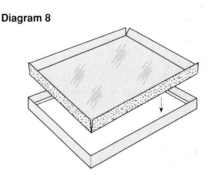

Repeat, applying the box lining to the inside of the box.

TERMS & TECHNIQUES

WORKING WITH PRINTED FABRICS

Before purchasing a printed fabric, study it carefully to determine if the print is a random design or if it has a repeating motif. If it has a repeating motif, you may need to purchase additional fabric to allow for matching.

To determine how much fabric to purchase:

- *Measure the distance between each repeat, as shown in **Diagram 1.***

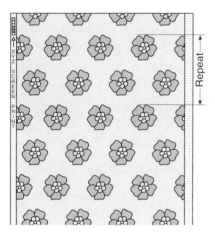

Diagram 1

- *Consult the appropriate "Cutting Directions" to determine the number of panels and/or ruffle sections for the project.*

- *Multiply the distance between each repeat by the number of panels and/or ruffle sections. Add this amount to the number of yards (meters) in the project's "Supplies" list.*

When cutting out the project, keep the following information in mind:

- *Cut adjoining panels or sections so that their upper edges fall at corresponding positions across the fabric's motif.*

- *Printed decorator fabrics are usually engineered so that the motifs can be matched by joining two widths just inside the selvage.*

- *If you are not using the full width of the fabric, match the panels along the seam line, as shown in **Diagram 2.***

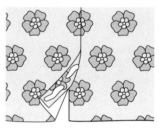

Diagram 2

To achieve an exact match when stitching the panels or sections together:

- *Referring to **Diagram 2,** press one seam allowance under along the seam line. Apply glue stick to the right side of the seam allowance. Lap the pressed seam allowance over the corresponding unpressed one, matching the seam lines and the fabric design.*

- *Turn the project sections to the wrong side, open out the folded seam allowance, and stitch along the creased line, as shown in **Diagram 3.***

Diagram 3

STITCHING TERMS

These are the stitching terms you'll find used throughout this book.

BACKSTITCHING

Backstitching is a machine stitching technique for securing the stitches at the beginning and end of a seam.

Insert the machine needle in the seam line about ⅜" (1cm) from the start of the seam. Lower the presser foot. Referring to **Diagram 4,** set the machine to sew in reverse and stitch to the edge of the fabric. Set the machine to stitch forward and stitch along the seam line to the end of the seam. Set the machine to stitch in reverse; backstitch for about ⅜" (1cm), stitching directly on top of the previous stitches.

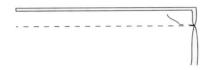

Diagram 4

CATCH STITCHING

Catch stitching is a hand-sewing technique that is used to hold two raw edges together.

Position the two edges so that they butt up against each other. Start at the left and secure the thread by taking a few small, tight stitches ¼" (6mm) below the edges. Referring to **Diagram 5** and inserting the needle from right to left, take a stitch to the right, above the edges. Repeat, taking the next stitch to the right, below the edges so that the stitches form an "×" Repeat, alternating the stitches approximately ¼" (6mm) above and below the edges and spacing the stitches approximately ¼" (6mm) apart.

Diagram 5

SLIP STITCHING

Slip stitching provides a neat, almost invisible way to secure two turned-under edges together by hand.

To begin, knot the end of the thread. Bury the knot in the fold of the fabric. Working from right to left and referring to **Diagram 6,** pick up a single fabric thread just below the folded edge. Insert the needle into the fold directly above the first stitch and bring it out ¼" (6mm) away. Pick up another single thread in the project directly below the point where the needle just emerged.

Diagram 6

RUFFLES

PREPARING A RUFFLE

Loosen the needle thread slightly. Machine baste along the raw edge of the ruffle, using two rows of stitches. Place the rows ¼" (6mm) and ¾" (2cm) from the edge and leave long thread tails at the beginning and end of the stitches, as shown in **Diagram 7.** Divide and mark the upper edge of the ruffle and the corresponding edge of the project into equal parts, according to the project's directions.

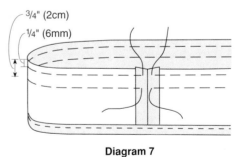

Diagram 7

GATHERING AND ATTACHING A RUFFLE

Pin the ruffle to the edge of the project, matching the markings.

Pull on the bobbin thread, drawing up the basting stitches. Gather the ruffle until it fits. Adjust the gathers so that they are evenly distributed between the markings. Stitch the ruffle to the project, placing the stitches ½" (1.3cm) from the raw edge of the ruffle, as shown in **Diagram 8.** Remove the basting stitches.

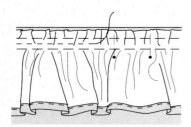

Diagram 8

APPLYING PIPING

Referring to **Diagram 9,** position the piping along the seam line on the right side of the fabric so that the raw edges are within the seam allowance and the piping cover's basting stitches are just inside the seam line. Using the machine zipper foot, machine baste the piping in place, stitching over the first row of basting stitches.

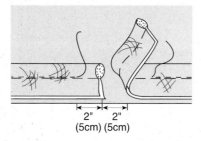

2" 2"
(5cm) (5cm)

Diagram 9

To join the ends, plan the joining to fall at an inconspicuous place on the project. Use a fabric marking pen to lightly mark the joining point.

- *Referring to **Diagram 9,** match the first end of the piping to the mark. Baste the piping in place, beginning 2" (5cm) from the mark. Baste around the project. Stop stitching 2" (5cm) before the mark, leaving the needle in the fabric and the presser foot down.*

- *Trim the piping so that the end will overlap the mark for 1" (2.5cm), as shown in **Diagram 10.***

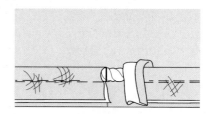

Diagram 10

- *Remove 1½" (3.8cm) of basting stitches from the overlap. Pull the piping cover back. Trim the filler cord so that it butts up against the other end of the cord at the mark. Turn the end of the piping cover under ½" (1.3cm). Wrap it around the exposed cord and the beginning of the piping. Finish basting the piping in place, as shown in **Diagram 11.***

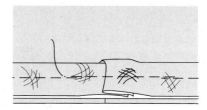

Diagram 11

To stitch a piped seam, position the project so that the section with the piping is on top. Stitch the seam, crowding the zipper foot up next to the piping so that all of the previous basting stitches will be concealed in the seam allowance, as shown in **Diagram 12.**

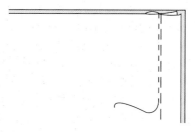

Diagram 12

MACHINE APPLIQUÉ

Adjust the sewing machine for a short, wide zigzag stitch. Use machine embroidery thread in the needle and all-purpose sewing thread in the bobbin.